Who Was Richard Haines,

the Quaker emigrant who died at sea in 1682?

Searching for his parents.

A narrative
by
Donna Haines Daly

Dedicated to all the other amateur genealogists out there.

In particular,
those who also descend from my Richard Haines

CONTENTS

Wills, Charts and Photographs

PREFACE

I must first acknowledge all the wonderful people who were there for me through this last quarter century of intense Haines research, beginning with my cousin, Eva, who generously got me started with her copy of Richard Haines' descendants in America, to Betty Kay for arranging the travel, to the helpful assistants at all the libraries and archives I visited, and to Susan for personal support and companionship on the annual BK Genealogy group trips as well as our one-time visit to archives and libraries in England. But mostly my children and grandchildren who have been extremely patient and amazingly helpful to the completion of this work.

I had two reasons for writing this treatise. The first being that my discovery of the birth of Richard's first son, John, and the previously unknown birth and death of a daughter, were discoveries of previously unknown or at least unpublished data, and certainly important enough to advertise, I thought. I wholeheartedly believe that every genealogist who has a Haines connection in his or her family tree will be interested in this writing, especially the thousands of descendants of Richard's eldest son John. Putting it out in the form of a printed book seemed at the time to be the safest way to get this information, this most important Haines discovery in a long time, out into the hinterlands of family history research while still claiming personal credit for the discovery.

The second reason was to make known the processes we genealogists go through while searching out elusive facts embedded in our histories. Processes which include repetitious reading of facts, going over the details again and again; while analyzing previous analyses, and thinking about various relationship possibilities and historical probabilities. I wanted to help the newbies, the budding family historians just beginning to research their family's past. It might give them an idea of possible starting points, or where to look when they hit the proverbial "brick wall." It might help someone to continue their search when it seems like there is no hope, or it might encourage some future Haines genealogist to prove or disprove some of the possibilities and probabilities that surfaced in my research and writing.

Also, and I think more importantly, we dedicated family historians have a tendency, nay, a deep need I think, to analyze, and to discuss our ongoing research with anyone who will listen. We seem to feel obliged to convey in detail each clue followed and each discovery eliminated, along with how it was found, where it was found, and why it was or was not worth saving. The exciting discoveries and the disheartening disappointments that occur in every genealogist's ongoing research always seem to be of utmost importance to that particular genealogist. And we want to tell someone. We mention names and dates and places and relationships that no one else can remember, keep track of, or care less about, all to the dismay of anyone who gets trapped into paying attention because they don't want to appear unkind or impolite. Unless it's a situation where help is requested, no one, and I mean *not one other person,* ever wants to hear any of it. Even the eyes of my closest family members appear to glaze over when I bring it up.

I became aware of this genealogical phenomenon many years ago when I found myself listening courteously to a boring lengthy story in which I was not the least bit interested, while desperately feeling a need to escape back into my own research. I didn't want to be rude and convey my true feelings, so I stayed and listened politely until I could nicely excuse myself. I was so put out by the situation that I vowed never to subject my friends to such misery, and consequently, whenever I'm asked how my research is going, I try to relate only the important highlights while leaving out boring (to them) details.

But I really do want to talk about it, I want to explain the possibilities and probabilities. I want to expound on the analyzing processes that went through my mind while in the throes of research. I want to talk about the excitement of each 'ah ha' moment and convey the depths of my disappointment at each failure. Writing this little book has allowed me to do just that, to go into great detail about every bit of it, and happily to relate that I did actually find some resolution. This tedious analyzation of the facts led me to find answers to many of the questions which had plagued my mind since the beginning of my research as well as questions that surfaced as a result of that research and analysis. It was truly a love affair with my English roots. I now leave it to the reader to peruse and enjoy its entirety or to focus only on the charts and factual details while skipping the boring analyzation.

Poulsbo, Washington, 2017   *Donna Haines Daly*

Curiosity 1

Sometime around 1990 I heard from a cousin that my paternal immigrant ancestor was Richard Haines, a Quaker who left England for America in 1682. Through diligent research of early Quaker records, this cousin had completed the American history and genealogy of our branch of the Haines family dating from 1682 in New Jersey to the 1700's in Virginia and Pennsylvania, to the 1800's in Ohio, Iowa and Oregon. But she had no information about Richard's life and family in England before 1682. I was curious. Where was he born? Who were his parents? Did he have siblings? Why did he leave England?

According to John W. Haines, whose most informative and well researched book about this family, *RICHARD HAINES and his descendants A Quaker Family of Burlington County, New Jersey since 1682*, the first record of Richard the immigrant is found in the Parish Records of St. Michael's Church, Aynhoe, Northamptonshire, England. This is where his sons, Richard, baptized 6 Aug 1665; Thomas, baptized 22 Dec 1666; and William, baptized 24 Apr 1672; were probably born. John W. Haines goes on to say that "sometime before 1665, and at some other place, Richard had married Margaret and they had had at least one other child", their eldest son, John. But no mention of these particular events can be found in the Aynhoe Parish Records. John W. Haines also said that the fact that Richard and Margaret continued to live in Aynhoe until leaving for America is evidenced by the birth record of their daughter, Mary in 1676, under the care of Banbury Monthly Meeting in Oxfordshire as well as a deed dated 21 April 1682, in which he gives his residence as Aynhoe. He tells us that Richard and Margaret, with their children, Richard, Thomas, William, and Mary,

> *left Aynhoe of Ye Hill in the spring of 1682....embarked at Gravesend, England, on the 'Amity' -- Richard Diamond, Master -- and sailed from Downs, England for West Jersey on April 23, 1682. The trip was long and tedious, as was common in the days of sailing ships. Richard, the father, sickened and died. After his death, another son, Joseph, was born on the high seas.*

I found the following somewhat romantic story of their 1682 Journey to America on the Internet, and it may or may not be all or partially true. The link identifying who posted the information went nowhere.

1682 Journey to America

This is the story of Richard Haines I and his family sailing to America aboard the Amity in 1682. The story was recorded in Joseph Haines Bible which was passed down in the Haines family for five generations to Dr. A. H. Stubbs in New Jersey.

Thus, from out of the yellowed pages, comes a story of heartaches, pathos and sadness, a tale that vividly depicts the harrowing circumstances that confronted the pioneers who braved wildernesses, oceans and savages in order to establish a home in the new world.

When Richard Haines sailed from England with his family in 1682 his hopes were bright and he looked forward with eagerness to the day when he would first behold the shores of America. That day never came, however, for he died during the voyage. His son, Joseph, born while his father was dying, lived to establish a long line of Haineses in the new world. Today his descendants are numerous in Lancaster county.

Like many other stories of colonial times, the adventure which ended so tragically for the elder Haines was closely linked with romance. His oldest son, John, then a youth of about twenty years of age, was ardently in love with Ester Borton, whose father, John Borton, was among earlier emigrants who came to America with their families in 1679.

The Haines and Bortons lived in the little village of Aynhoe-On-The-Hill, County of Northampton, England, and neither John or Ester dreamed that their romance was shortly to be tragically interrupted. Ester's father, however, was determined to seek his fortune in the new world and Richard Haines signed his certificate of removal despite his son's pleading.

The parting between the lovers was pathetic and before the final words of farewell were spoken, John promised to follow her to the new world as soon as circumstances permitted.

John Borton settled in America three years after West Jersey was assigned to William Penn and others for the benefit of the creditors of Edward Byllings, who, with John Fenwick, had purchased the interests of Lord Berkeley. Sir George Cartoret retained the eastern part of the province which was known as East Jersey while that held by Penn was known as West Jersey.

Life from then on was an endless dream to Ester Borton who went about her daily tasks with a sorrowful heart, wishing and hoping for the day when her lover would sail the seas and they could be together again. A year went past before John left England. During those long, tortuous months, many exciting incidents happened in the little colony.

The Quaker proprietors gave the settlers a remarkable liberal constitution of government and soon many emigrants from England and from other provinces, notably Long Island, flocked to West Jersey to find repose and peace. Many, like Borton, came with the purpose of building a new home and acquiring ultimate financial gain in the new world, but they encountered difficulties by reason of the detested methods employed by the viceroy Andros.

They found that the peace and repose they had anticipated was not to be enjoyed by lovers of freedom "anywhere under royal rule." They also were impressed with the injunction "Put not your trust in princes" for King James of England failed to keep the promises made by the Duke of York and they were compelled to submit to the tyranny of Andros.

These were the conditions which confronted John Haines when, in 1680 he finally reached America and joined his sweetheart, Ester Borton. Life in the new world was full of promise, however, despite the many happenings that marred the otherwise happy existence of the early settlers.

Within a short time the elder Haines received letters containing glowing accounts of his son's new home and the wonderful future the country held for those who were willing to labor in search of it. Finally, in 1682, his father, inspired by the information contained in the letters, determined to cast lots with his son and sailed from Gravesend with his wife and four children on the ship "Amity."

Prior to his leaving England, Richard Haines had obtained two grants of land in West Jersey, presumably in the same county, Burlington, wherein his son resided.

The "Amity" was a slow-moving sailing vessel of the type then prevalent. Her captain was Richard Diamond, a veteran, whose father had been a captain before him. In her hold, the "Amity" carried various commodities which were assured of a ready sale in America—dried beef, silks and satins, rum and tea.

No premonition of impending tragedy presented itself as the ship, her sails billowing to the breeze, slowly moved away from the dock, while friends of those on board shouted their last farewells and wished the travelers "Bon Voyage."

Sailing ships in those days, were at the mercy of the elements and shortly after leaving England a storm of great intensity swept from the west and engulfed the ship. As the night wore on the waves mounted to gigantic proportions and soon the ship was completely off her course.

After weeks, during which the "Amity" valiantly fought her way across the ocean, provisions ran low. The women and children were given preference in the matter of the little remaining food while the water, much of which had become fetid and germ ladened, was rigidly apportioned so that it would last until land was reached.

Then, when all danger seemed to have been averted and hopes had again taken the place of despair in the minds of the voyagers, Richard Haines was suddenly stricken. His wife, Margaret, was unable to assist him and he lay for days in a stupor.

His children, crowding about him, prayed that he might get well but Fate decreed otherwise and he died while the ship was still many miles from the coast.

Saddened by his death, certain of the passengers staid by the bedside of his wife while the ship lurched in the troughs of waves seemed intent upon adding to the misery and suffering the circumstances had produced. A few hours later her child was born.

A few days before the ship made port the baby was christened Joseph in the presence of the passengers and members of the crew. Even during those trying days, when only a little food remained, the Christian spirit of those hardy pioneers was manifested by the intensity of their prayers and the deeply religious spirit portrayed during the christening.

The ship finally reached the shores of America and Mrs. Haines, with her four children and new-born babe, hastened to the home of her son, John, where she lived for some years. Here her son Joseph grew to manhood. Here in an environment where sturdiness and courage were demanded at every turn, he received the rudiments of learning which were all the place afforded.

His mother taught him in her spare moments, but these were few and far between.

Conditions in the little Jersey colony were not of the best. Winters were long and caused much suffering. A few years before Mrs. Haines reached America Sir George Cartoret died and the trustees of his estate offered East Jersey for sale. It was bought in 1682, the year Joseph was born, by William Penn and others, among them the Earl of Perth, the friend of Robert Barclay, whom the proprietors appointed governor of the domain for life.

Barclay was an eminent young man whose writings have been held in high estimation by his sect, especially his "Apology for the true Christian Divinity." The purchase was made not in the interest of religion or liberty, but as a land speculation which was not in accord with the wishes of many of the settlers.

The "viceroy" Andros especially made himself hated by the Jersey pioneers and when that detested individual was driven from the country in 1689 the domain was left without a regular civil government for many years.

Wearied with the contentions with the people of the provinces and with the government in England and annoyed by losses in unprofitable speculations, the proprietors of the Jerseys finally surrendered them to the crown in 1702 when Queen Anne was the reigning British monarch.

The government of the domain was then confided to Sir Edward Hyde, whose instructions constituted the supreme law of the land. He was then governor of New York and possessed almost absolute legislative and executive control within the jurisdiction of his authority.

In New Jersey the people had no voice in the judiciary or in the making and executing of laws other than recommendatory. Liberty of conscience was granted to all but those of the Catholic faith, but the bigoted governor always showed conspicuous favors to the members of Church of England. Under his rule the people of New Jersey were slaves. Printing was prohibited in the province except by royal permission and the traffic of Negro slaves was especially encouraged.

The province of New Jersey remained a dependency of New York with a distinct legislative assembly of its own until the year 1738 when through the efforts of Lewis Morris, its chief justice, it was made an independent colony and so continued until the Revolutionary War.

It was amid such conditions that the youthful Joseph Haines passed the early years of his life, conditions that brought out his innate spirit of adventure. Eventually he became restless and wishing to strike out for himself, he left his home in New Jersey and journeyed westward through the primeval wilderness of colonial Pennsylvania and settled in Nottingham township, Chester County.

For many years the man who had entered the world under such harrowing circumstances served as a justice-of-the-peace in the little settlement wherein he had taken up his abode. His son, Job, who was born August 26, 1744 married Ester Kirk.

Timothy Haines, Job's son married Sarah Brown on March 12, 1795 and moved to Fulton township, Lancaster County. He died January 2, 1842 and his son, Timothy Jr. Married Rachel E. Kirk, whose daughter, Sarah B. was the wife of Charles H. Stubbs, father of the late Dr. AH. Stubbs of Penn Hill.

THE FRIENDS, OR QUAKERS
Pennsylvania, the Quaker Colony, was founded by William Penn in 1681,under a patent granted by Charles II on March 4th, 1681. The first colony left England in August 1681, in three ships, the John and Sarah, from London, the Amity, from London, and the Factor from Bristol. The John and Sarah is said too have landed first; the Amity was carried by a gale to the West Indies; and the Factor, having proceeded up the Delaware as far as the present town of Chester, was on December 11, frozen up in the channel and its passengers obliged to pass the winter there. William Penn had sent his cousin William Markham with the colonists as deputy governor, and did not emigrate himself until the month of August 1682 when he embarked on the 'WELCOME". After a passage of some two months, during which smallpox broke out among the emigrants, and carried off one-third of their number, Penn and his fellow colonists landed at Newcastle, Del. on Oct 27, 1682. Of the history of Penn's colony, and of Quaker government during the next 93 years and until it was finally overthrown in 1776 by the Revolutionary Scotch-Irish, it is not necessary here to speak. The influence of the Quakers in the settlement and growth of the states south of Pennsylvania, has never been sufficiently recognized. It was from these states that most of the Quaker emigrants to Harrison and adjacent counties, Virginia came.

John W. Haines wrote that Richard Haines was a man of some means as he was able to purchase land in America before leaving England, that Richard and Margaret's oldest son John preceded his parents to America in 1679, and that

John was undoubtedly instrumental in his parents deciding to leave England. West Jersey, in America, through the influence of William Penn and others was being settled largely by members of the Society of Friends, the religious group Richard had joined sometime between 1672 when his son, William, was baptized at Aynhoe, and 1676 when his daughter, Mary, was baptized under the care of the Banbury Monthly Meeting of the Society of Friends. With their children, Richard, Thomas, William, and Mary, Richard and Margaret Haines left England in the spring of 1682. They embarked at Gravesend on the 'Amity' and sailed from Downs, England for West Jersey on 23 April 1682.

Margaret and her family arrived at Burlington, New Jersey in the fall of that year, and information about how she and her children lived and managed in this new and wild country without a husband and father is unknown. But since she was a devout member of the Society of Friends, a group of religious dissenters known for their practice of caring for each other and doing good works in the community, it is probably safe to assume that they managed well enough. After about two and one half years, on 3 May 1685, at Thomas Gardiner's house in Burlington, New Jersey, under the care of Burlington Monthly Meeting, Margaret Haines married Henry Burcham of Neshamony, Bucks Co., Pennsylvania. No record of what happened to daughter Mary has yet been discovered.

This Richard Haines has been researched and written about over and over again by untold numbers of genealogists, the most important one being the above mentioned John W. Haines in 1961. In none of these writings or published accounts have I found any provable evidence of the identity of Richard's parents or the birth of his son John. Several totally incorrect names and places of residence have been assigned to Richard's parents on the Internet. One in particular seems to be everywhere, a John Hayne and Elizabeth Stanford of Rudgewick in Sussex County. I found this to be totally incorrect when on page 164 of *SUSSEX GENEALOGIES* Compiled by John Comber, in paragraph IV, was written:

> *JOHN HAYNE. Bp. 11 Mch. 1608/9. Disinherited by father. Bur 12 June 1664. Marr 9 May 1639 or 40, Elizabeth Stanford. [Bur 9 Aug 1684] and had issue:--*
>   *? Edward Hayne. Bur 13 Apr 1668*
>   *Abraham Hayne. Bp. 9 Aug 1649.*
>   *John Hayne. Bp. 8 June 1652.*
>   *Isaac Hayne (V).*
>   *Mary. Bp. 12 May 1642.*

This couple with their known children's names and birth dates made their parenting of my Richard impossible. Not to mention that Sussex County is some distance from the last place he was proven by John W. Haines to be, which was as a member of Banbury Monthly Meeting in Oxfordshire County and Aynho Parish in Northamptonshire County, about six miles southeast of Banbury.

First Astounding Discoveries

2

In 1995 on my first trip to the Family History Library in Salt Lake City I began looking for Richard's parents. While searching through records of baptisms in Newbottle Parish on Fiche #6128147, to which I had been directed by the helper at the desk who recommended the index of surnames, I came across a notation written in Latin that read

Anna Heyns filia Rchrd et Margret de Charlton

"Was this my Richard and Margaret?" I wondered. "No, it can't be," I thought. First because it was too easy to find. After all, if I could find it so quickly others could too, and surely would have if it were correct. Second, because Heyns was not spelled correctly, and number three, my Richard did not have a daughter named Anna. Only John, born in some other part of England, and his brothers, Richard, Thomas, and William, all baptized at Aynhoe; and daughter, Mary, at Banbury Monthly Meeting. So I gave up and decided to try breaking down some American 'brick walls' elsewhere in the Haines line. That was somewhat successful. I did find some names and dates I had previously been unaware of to fill in previous records. But when all those little easy discoveries dried up I gave in, left that search, and went to the International floor where I researched my Norwegian roots.

In the Norwegian bookshelves I found one book, *The Slektsbok for Sørfold*, which had my maternal grandfather's name and siblings listed with their parents and the name of the farm I knew he had been born on; but it was written in Norwegian and I could not figure out how to use the information. Later that year, I went to Norway, and there at the home of a second cousin, I found the same book. With the help of Norwegian relatives who speak fluent English, I was finally able to understand it. For the next three years, until I found enough to satisfy my curiosity, I gleaned all the information I could on the Norway floor of the Family History Library. I even traveled to Norway to search the Norwegian National Archives at Hamar where I found information that was not available at the Family History Library. And to Trondheim, where most of the information in their books was available in Salt Lake City. I then tried again to break down those American 'brick walls' with absolutely no success.

It was in 2001 when I decided to try again to find my Richard's parents. Back down on the British floor of the Family History Library, I found through use of the card catalogue, a Richard and Margaret Haines who had sons John, Richard and Thomas. "Here it is" I thought. This must be my Richard and Margaret. On Film #0416750, which held the parish records of Fittleworth in Sussex County, I found the marriage at Fittleworth of "Rich Haines and Margaret Philps of Petworth". But this information proved to be unrelated to my family when, after more trips to Salt Lake City searching parish records of Fittleworth and Petworth, I found the birth dates of their sons, John, Richard and Thomas, dates which proved to be at odds with the birth dates of my John, Richard and Thomas. My next exciting discovery was on film #1364154. A marriage at Finden, also in Sussex County, of John Hayne and Margaret Breaden on 8 Jun 1637. An appropriate year for the parents of my Richard Haines to have married, I thought. But this couple also had children whose names were different and who were born on the wrong dates.

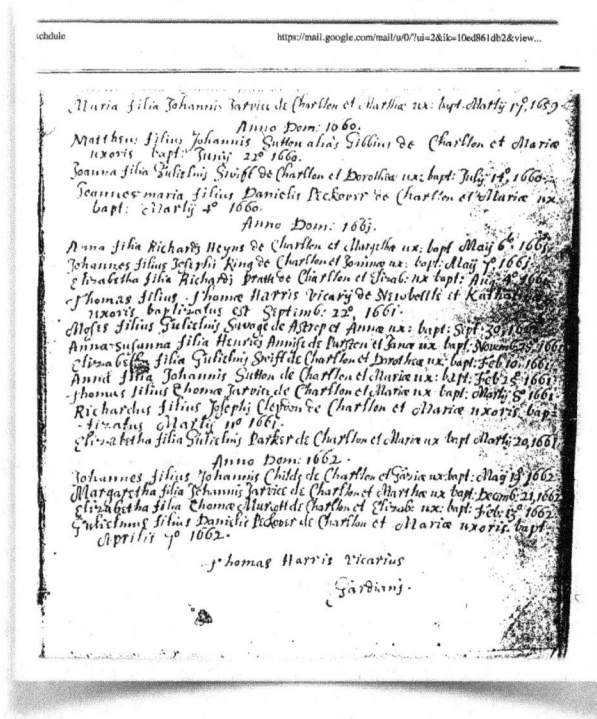

I kept looking, and it was those same parish records that I had rejected on my first trip to Salt Lake City that opened it all up for me. On June 22, 2005, while perusing the almost indecipherable old English writing on fiche #6128147, which contained the records of Newbottle Parish, I again found myself looking at:

ANNA filia Richardus Heyns de Charlton et Margetha ux: bapt May 6,1661.

This still made no sense to me, but I continued with these difficult records, hoping to find some small bit of data that fit what I already knew about my Richard and Margaret. After ten years or so of reading Norwegian and Old English records, I found it a little easier to make out the words. I had also become more open-minded about accepting data that seemed pertinent to my family research but failed to fit my expectations perfectly. Finally, on that same fiche, #6128147, I did see two more important lines on other pages which made sense. The first being

JOHANNES filius Richardus Heyns de Charlton, et Margat: ux: bapt: Jul 24, 1663.

Oh! What excitement! Surely, I thought, this must be the first son of my Richard and Margaret, the one John W. Haines said was "born at some other place." And on a later page of these same records I found the second line.

ANNA HEYNS de Charlton Sepulta Marty 12, 1668

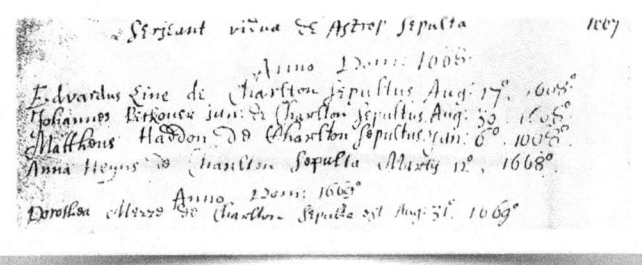

Oh my God! I thought. She died! No wonder she had never been discovered. She lived only 6 years 10 months. My Richard's first son, John, had been born almost two years after their first daughter. Here in these Newbottle parish records were the first and second children of my Richard and Margaret Haines, a previously unknown daughter, Anna, and their eldest son John, who had up until that moment been known only as the son who was born "at some other place" and had emigrated two years before his family. Then it hit me. It was more feeling than fact, but I seemed to know for sure! These were my people. Apparently none of the previous researchers had looked at, or at least never published, information from the Newbottle records, and therefore never found John's birth or Anna's baptism and burial at Charlton.

After the initial excitement, I settled down and surmised that if Anna was born in 1661, then Richard and Margaret probably married in 1659 or 1660, and probably at the same place John and Anna were born. That shouldn't be too hard. After all I had been able to make out the writing for Anna and John's births, so if I was really diligent and careful I could find their parent's marriage, couldn't I? I did find the marriage pages, and looked for the year 1660. At the top of page 31 was the title

NUPTIA ANNO DOM: 1650

which means "marriages performed in the year 1650." Several lines down the page appeared three more such titles followed by *Nulla Nuptia hoc anno celebrate* with no names between.

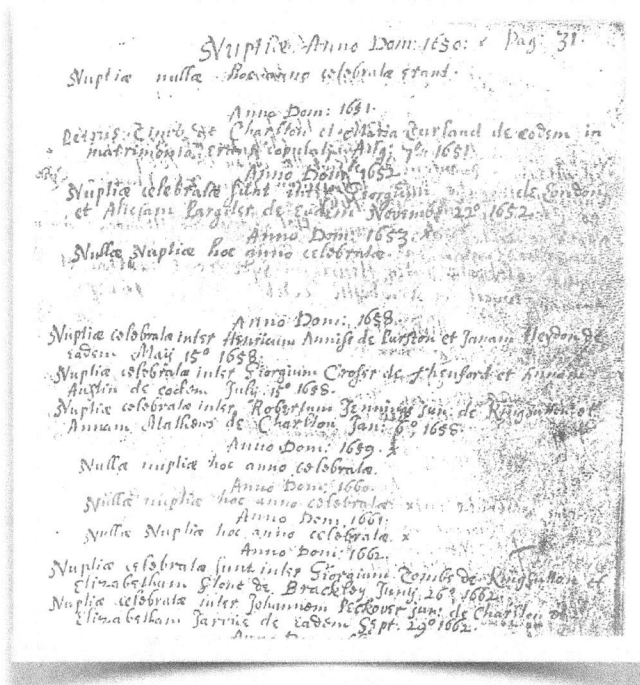

Anno Dom: 1659
Nulla Nuptia hoc anno
celebrate

Anno Dom: 1660
Nulla Nuptia hoc anno
celebrate"

Anno Dom 1661
Nulla Nuptia hoc anno
celebrate

The English meaning of that Latin phrase is "no marriages to celebrate this year". And then for 1662 it goes on to list several couples. But no Heyns, Heynes, Haynes, or Haines. So I continued the wider search for evidence of any record which might connect to my Richard.

I studied gazetteers, maps, county histories, court records and parish records. I looked at every Richard and John Haines/Hanes/Haynes/Heines/Heynes/Henes born about the right time and listed in any index or transcript in and around Southern Northamptonshire and Northern Oxfordshire, areas around the last place my Richard was known to be. I looked for a John Haines because of what appeared to be the naming patterns at that time, that the first son usually had his paternal grandfather's given name.   And my Richard had named his first son John.

Banbury and Aynhoe are about six miles apart on the border between these two counties, as are Newbottle Parish and Charlton, also nearby. Newbottle Parish includes portions of Astrop and Charlton with other portions being in Kings Sutton, a manor which will later prove to have connections to my Richard. *Kings Sutton Churchwardens's Accounts 1636-1700,* compiled by The Banbury Historical Society validates this on the first page:

> *The parish of Kings Sutton covered both the village of Kings Sutton, which then had a population of about 500-600, and also the hamlets of Astrop and Walton and parts of Purston and Charlton.   Other parts of Purston and Charlton were in the parish of Newbottle.*

Charlton is bounded on the north by Farthingham and Middleton Cheney, on the east by Hinton, on the south by Aynhoe and on the west by Kings Sutton. The village of Newbottle is 4 miles southeast of Banbury.

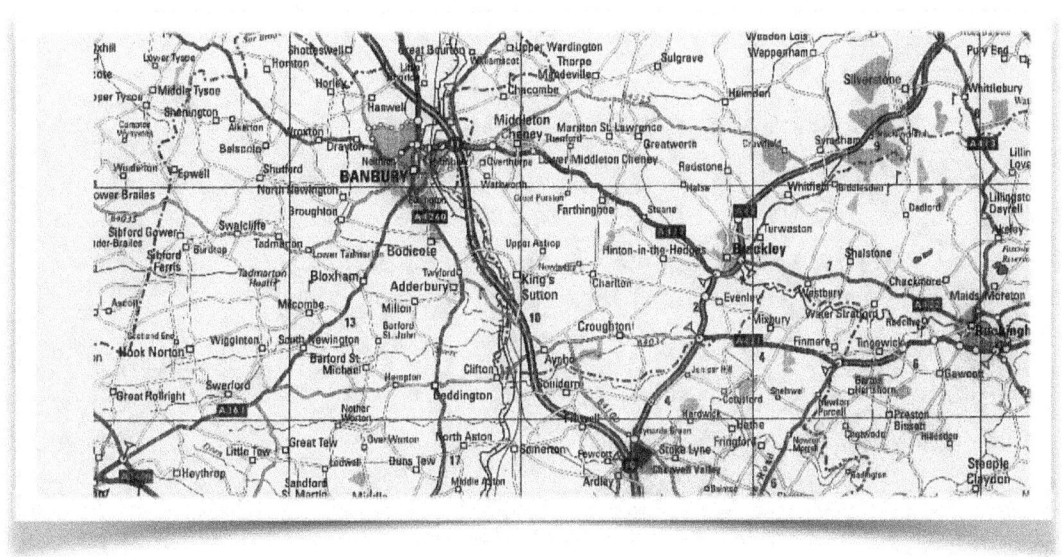

Meaningful Olde Wills

3

I was struggling through one more microfilm of old records, this one being film #0092127-40, court records written in old English and equally difficult to decipher, when I happened upon the name Marie Heynes written clearly in the margin of one page with the year 1633 written directly below the name. It was very small but legible, and I immediately went to make a paper copy of this will written in old English. I would find a helper at the desk who could read it for me and my tape recorder.

In the name of God, Amen, the four and twentieth day of October, I Mary Heynes of Kings Sutton, in the county of Northampton, widow, being in bodily health and in good memory do ordain and make this my last will and testament in form and manner following: first I commit my soul into the hands of almighty god who gave the same unto me. Offering myself by the merit, death and passion of Christ Jesus his only son and my redeemer to be saved and my body to the earth from where it came until that great day of our resurrection when the lord shall call me and all other from the same by the trump of his angels, and the same to be buried in the church of Kings Sutton.

Item: I give and bequeath unto my eldest son Richard Haines, the table in the hall with the frame and the benches and the cupboard in the hall, also I give unto him the joined bedstead over the hall in my chamber, my great panne, my malt mill, my chestern, the house thru(?sic), a woolen bolster, two pieces of pewter, one pair of sheets, one blanket, one featherbed, and after the decease of him unto his son William, the featherbed.

Item: I do give unto my son Thomas Haines one feather bolster, a blanket, a pair of sheets, two pieces of pewter, one pillow homemade.

Item: I give unto Anne Smith my daughter, one coverlid, a feather pillow a bolster with wool the long cover, two pieces of pewter, one pair of sheets, advik(?sic) barrel, a brass kettle last bought, a yearling cow, and in money five pounds.

Item: I give unto Susanna Toms, my daughter, one pair of sheets, one blanket, a pillow of feathers, a bolster with wool, the great kettle, the least pot, a meshing fat(?sic), .. the card(?sic) dough cover, five pieces of pewter, the bed in the high chamber.

Item: I do give unto Elizabeth Smith and Mary Smith, my grandchildren, each of them one mattress.

ITEM: I give unto Anne Smith my grandchild the bright panne.

Item: I give unto everyone of my grandchildren 3 shillings apiece.

Item: I give unto the poor of Kings Sutton 10 shillings.

Item: I do give unto the maintaining of the bells 2 shillings. All the rest of my goods unbequeathed I give unto son, John Haines, making him my whole executor. My debts and legacies discharged lastly I do ordain my brother Thomas Pargiter and John Pargiter to be overseers of this my last will and testament and I give them for their pains 2 shillings.

Marie Haines her mark

witnesses of this my last will and testament
John Pargiter
Alexander Smith

See Family chart following:

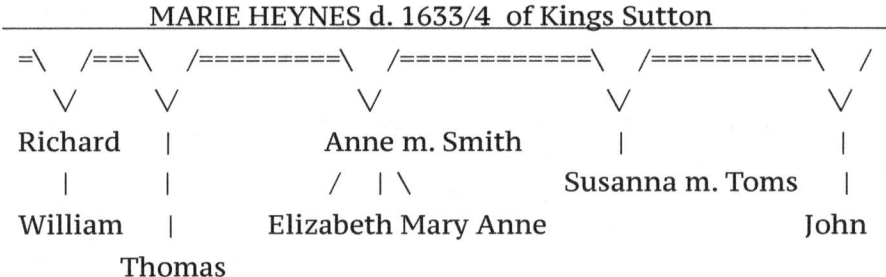

Oh, the thrill, the excitement of this 'aha' moment. Marie Heynes of Kings Sutton who mentioned sons Richard, Thomas and John, might be related to me. My Richard named his boys John, Richard, Thomas, and William. Marie's son Richard would not have been born at the right time to actually be my ancestor, but any of his sons might have been. Richard could have had sons named John and Richard born at the right time. Or, more likely, Marie's son, John, could have been the father of my Richard. And Marie had mentioned brothers Thomas and John Pargiter. So Marie's maiden name was Pargiter. I wondered, was this Marie (Pargiter) Heynes the grandmother of my Richard? Perhaps I could find records of Marie's sons, Richard and John, with wives and children.

I looked up Kings Sutton in *The Phillimore Atlas and Index of Parish Registers*, and found it on the map of Northamptonshire, located partly on an eminence, about three miles southeast of Banbury near Newbottle and Charlton.(See map p. 13)

Kings Sutton Parish Church

There were many John and Richard Hayneses right there in Kings Sutton and in every other small village within a fifteen mile radius, but none seemed to fit the time frame and family pattern necessary to make them mine.

I went through many more records and found a will for a Richard Haines of Helmdon dated 1656 on microfilm #187571. Definitely not my Richard, but I thought he could be connected somehow. I copied the will and went to the Phillimore Gazetteer to find that Helmdon Parish contained three manors, and that the Village of Helmdon is situated partly in a valley about ten miles west of Banbury.

Will of Richard Haines

In the name of God Amen the six and twentieth day of March in the year of our lord God One thousand six hundred fifty and six   I Richard Haines of

Helmdon in the county of Northampton, laborer, being sick in body but of good and perfect memory thanks be given to almighty God herefore do make and ordain this my last will and testament in manner and form following

... first I give and bequeath my soul unto God the creator and maker of all things and to Jesus Christ the redeemer of all mankind and to the holy ghost the sanctifier of all the elect people of God of which number I steadfastly believe myself to be one and to be saved by the merits of the death of my lord and savior Jesus Christ and by none other and my body to be buried in the churchyard of Helmdon or elsewhere it should please God.

Item: I give unto my beloved wife, Em (Emma) Haines my house wherein I now dwell with all the backside and close thereto belonging during the time of her widowhood and I also give unto my said wife the use of all my goods during her widowhood and after the marrying or death of my said wife the first that shall happen I give and bequeath my said house with the backside and close and mounds thereto belonging unto my second son Richard Haines his heirs and assigns forever. Always provided that If my said son Richard Haines do happen to die and depart out of this life without any lawful heir of his body that then in such case my said house, backside and close with their appurtenances shall be equally divided betwixt my younger son Wm Haines and so many of my daughters as shall be then living to remain to them their heirs and assigns forever. My son William shall have no more part than one of his sisters but they shall all have parts alike.

Item: I give and bequeath unto my eldest son Thomas Haines 2 shillings 6 pense of lawful english money to be paid unto him immediately after my decease if he come for it.

Item: I give unto my daughter Jone 20 shillings lawful english money

Item I give unto my daughter Em 20 shillings lawful english money

Item: I give unto my daughter Mary 20 shillings of lawful english money

Item: I give unto my daughter Alice 2 shillings 6 pense of lawful english money to be paid unto her presently after my decease if it be demanded

Item: I give unto daughter Hester 20 shillings of lawful english money

Item: I give unto my daughter Margery 20 shillings of lawful english money

Item: I give unto my son William Haines 20 shillings of lawful english money. my will is that these six children which I have given 20 shillings apiece unto shall be paid by my executor the eldest of them shall be paid within one year after my decease and the next eldest within two years after and so to be paid one more year til they all be paid according to their age.

And I do make and appoint my second son Richard Haines to be sole executor of this my present testament. In witness whereof I have to this my last will and testament set my hand and seal the day and year above written.

Signed sealed published in the presence of
Wm. Cross
Borton
Alse Haines

          (signed)   Richard Haines

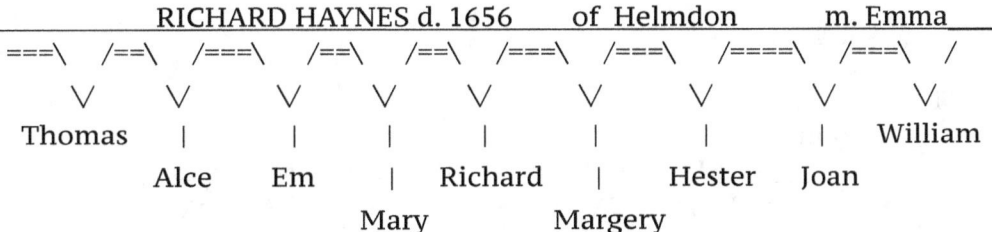

I believe this Richard may be the eldest son of the aforementioned Marie and Thomas Heynes. He named his first son Thomas after his father and his second son Richard after his grandfather and himself, as tradition seemed to dictate at that time. But if he was the eldest son, why was he living at Helmdon? Why not Kings Sutton where his mother had been located?

If this Richard of Helmdon was, in fact, Marie and her husband Thomas's eldest son, he should have inherited his father's copyhold land at Kings Sutton upon his father's death--if his father had owned or had a tenancy on any of that land. According to Peter B. Park in *MY ANCESTORS WERE MANORIAL TENANTS,* this old traditional system of primogeniture would also have given Thomas's widow, Marie, the right to live there by dower and

> *enjoy use or benefits of the whole of her late husband's estate for the rest of her natural life, before it passes on to his heir.*

Although Marie was a resident of Kings Sutton when she died, and may have been living there by dower, I have yet to find evidence of any ownership, copyhold, or tenancy of Thomas's. But it could still exist somewhere in the old records. Park also says that

> *a married woman (who is an heiress) could not be a tenant (on her own land), her husband held the tenancy in the right of his wife. And on her death the tenancy passed to her heir.*

And her heir, according to *The Records of Knowle,* mentioned later in this writing, would have been her "youngest son, and for want of a son, her youngest daughter." This means that Richard's mother, Marie (Pargiter) Heynes, if she was the youngest child of a previous copyhold or tenancy owner, would have been heir to that part of Kings Sutton, and it would have gone to her youngest child upon the death of her husband, Thomas. (See chart following.)

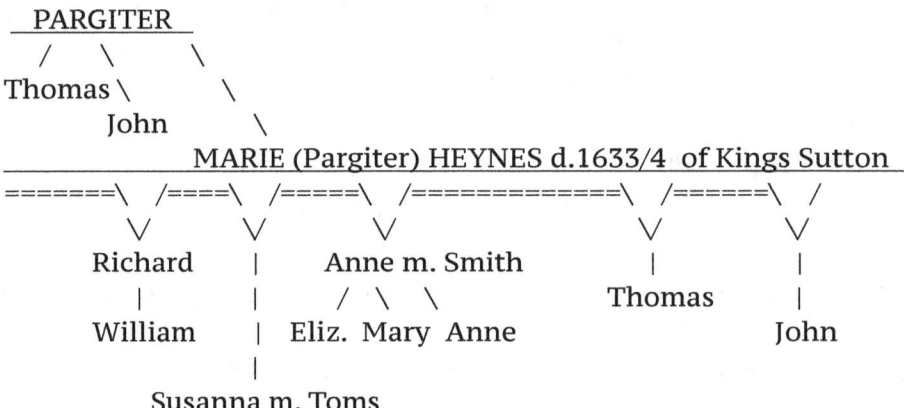

This also would have given her the right to live there by dower until her own demise. But Richard was not her youngest son, and neither was he Thomas's heir. Therefore, he apparently did not inherit any of Kings Sutton. I wonder. Who did inherit the tenancy at Kings Sutton? Was it Marie's son John? He was her named executor. And he would have been the right age to be father to my Richard. But why do I find no marriage or burial records for him, or children's baptisms?

Why was the eldest son, Thomas, left only two shillings and six pence in Richard of Helmdon's will? His wording in the will regarding Thomas, "*if he come for it,*" eludes my understanding at this time. The eldest son should inherit his father's property.

Perhaps Richard's wife, Emma, who he named in his will, had been heiress to property and the tenancy on the Manor at Helmdon at the time of their marriage. He did leave it all to her in his will. That could be the reason Richard did not consider himself a yeoman, but claims in his will, to be a laborer. Possibly since his wife, Emma, was still living but could only live there by dower, not as a tenant, Richard willed his *house wherein (he dwelt) with all the backside and close thereto belonging...also...use of all (his) goods during her widowhood and after the marrying or death of (his) said wife the first that shall happen I give and bequeath (my) said house and backside and close and mounds thereto belonging unto (my) second son Richard Haines his heirs and assigns forever.*

If Emma was an heiress, Richard would have had 'free bench' to her inherited property at Helmdon, and her youngest son would have inherited the tenancy upon Richard's death. Emma was probably mother to Richard's second son Richard, and he must have been her youngest son to be considered heir to his mother's tenancy. In his will, Richard calls William his 'younger son', but apparently he is not Emma's 'younger son' or he would have been the one to inherit. This would be true unless the Manor of Helmdon did not have the "youngest son or for want of a son, the youngest daughter" rule to inherit as it was in the Manor of Knowle. (See possibility charted following with the children of Richard and Emma in bold print and Richard's other children in regular print.)

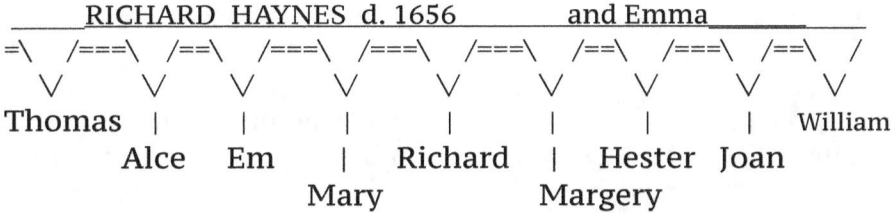

As to why Richard's eldest son, Thomas, was left only two shillings and six pence in the will; perhaps he had a different mother. Richard's eldest son, Thomas, may have been the youngest son of a deceased first wife who had been heiress to a tenancy elsewhere, or he may have been illegitimate. Richard said also of a bequest to his daughter, Alice, "if it be demanded." This also eludes my understanding. (See Richard and unknown mother of Thomas and Alse in bold print charted below.)

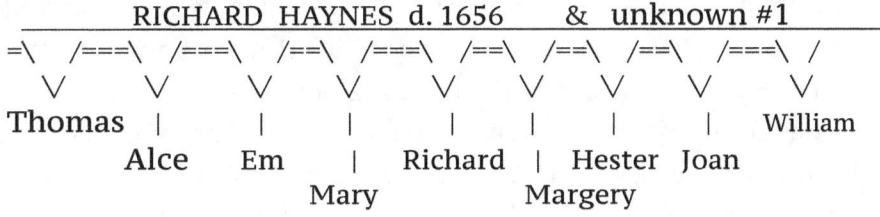

There seems to be no explanation for why this Richard's son, William, inherited only money like the girls. He may also have been illegitimate.

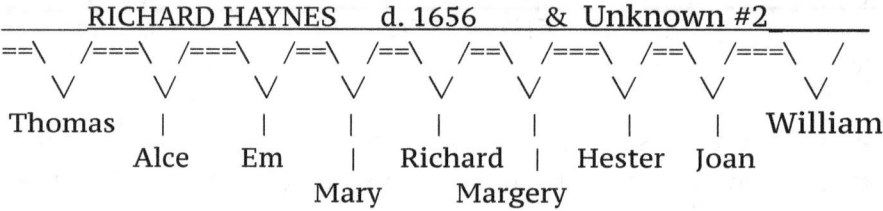

RICHARD HAYNES   d. 1656   & Unknown #2

Thomas | | | | | | | William
Alce   Em | Richard | Hester Joan
Mary   Margery

Marie Heynes, in her 1633 will, bequeathed furniture and household items to her eldest son, Richard, and after his decease, to his son, William. Twenty three years later, this Richard of Helmdon leaves only 20 shillings to his son, William. But if this William were the same William mentioned in Marie's will, he should have been the eldest, having been mentioned in a will twenty three years earlier.

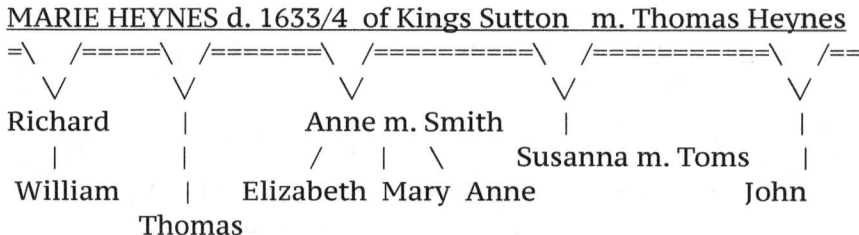

MARIE HEYNES d. 1633/4 of Kings Sutton   m. Thomas Heynes

Richard | Anne m. Smith | |
| | / | \ Susanna m. Toms |
William | Elizabeth Mary Anne John
Thomas

Perhaps the William mentioned in 1633 by Marie had since died, and another William had been born to Richard. Or, it is also possible that this Richard Haines of Helmdon is not the eldest son of Marie and Thomas Heynes of Kings Sutton.

On my 2013 trip to England to visit the Northampton Public Record Offices where my people might be found, I searched/copied all the Helmdon records available and found little to fit my family. There was a Thomas and Anne Haynes having children from 1619 to 1633, and this could have been Richard's eldest son, Thomas. There was a Henry and Alice Haynes having children from 1658 to 1663, but Richard did not mention a son, Henry in his will. He did mention a daughter, Alice, who may have married a Henry Haynes. There was also a Richard and Catherine Haynes having children from 1669 to 1672. This could be the second son Richard mentions in his will, but I cannot fit him anywhere into my family.

According to the following 1606 will of Elizabeth Haynes of Kings Sutton, a widow who may also have been living by dower on her late husband's copyhold land; which I found on film #173601 at the Family History Library in Salt Lake City in Jan 2006, Marie Heynes, who died in 1634, was apparently the widow of Elizabeth's son Thomas Heynes. Elizabeth mentions a Richard Haynes, son of her son Thomas Haynes. This means that Richard of Helmdon, if he was Marie's son, would have been at least sixty years old when he died in 1656.

Will of Elizabeth Heynes, proven 18 Jan 1607.

17 October, 1606

In the name of God Amen, I Elizabeth Haynes of Kings Sutton in the county of Northamptonshire widow sick of body but in perfect mind and remembrance give thanks to almighty God . I ordain this my last will and testament in manner and form following. First: I surrender my soul into the hands of almighty God desiring the salvation thereof in Jesus Christ. Thanks be to almighty God I ordain this my last will and testament in manner and form following. ...Jesus Christ ;... and my body to be buried in the churchyard of Kings Sutton above said.

Item: I give unto Richard Haynes, son to Thomas Haynes my son my red cow and pair of sheets, a mattress, two yellow ...hillings a brass ...

Item: I give to John Haynes, son also to my son Thomas Haynes 20 shillings of current english money.

Item: I give unto Thomas Haynes son also to my son Thomas Haynes a pair of ...balee.(sic) and one bushel of malt.

Item: I give to Anne Haynes daughter to Thomas Haines my son one pair of sheets , a christening sheet, the best silver spoon, ...table cloth .., the best pillow case, a table napkin, a kettle, a comb?... a table cloth .. a feather bedd...

Item I give to Sarah Baylee, daughter to my daughter Alce Haynes a feather bedd, a pair of sheets, a christening sheet, the next best to Anne Haynes a towel, a table napkin, a kerchief, a ... tablecloth, a hilling?, a bolt of..., a kettle with a bale, a blanket, to Anne Haines twelve (money).

Item: I give to Michael Baylee my daughter Alce her son XX (20) shillings of english currency

Item: to Richard Haines my son's son 5 shillings in money and also to Thomas Haynes his brother, 5 shillings.

Item I give to the abovesaid Anne Haines one platte, .

Item I give to the said Sarah Baylee one platte

Item: I give to Susan Haynes daughter to my son Thomas Haynes one whole calf, a pair of best sheets, a towel, a table napkin, a table cloth,

Item I give to the above named Richard Haines the brass pot, a ... platte a table napkin.

chattels debt and whatsoever is unbequeathed I give to my son Thomas Haynes who I ordain executor of this my last will and testament to ... pr...

I do appoint overseers of this said will Thomas Swaine of Sutton and Mr. James Smith vicar of Sutton abovesaid and I give them for their pains VI (6) pence apiece. Item: I give to my daughter Dorothy her children XII d. (12 pence) apiece.

witnesses: James Smith   Thomas Swaine
Elizabeth Haynes her mark
proven 18 day of Jan 1607

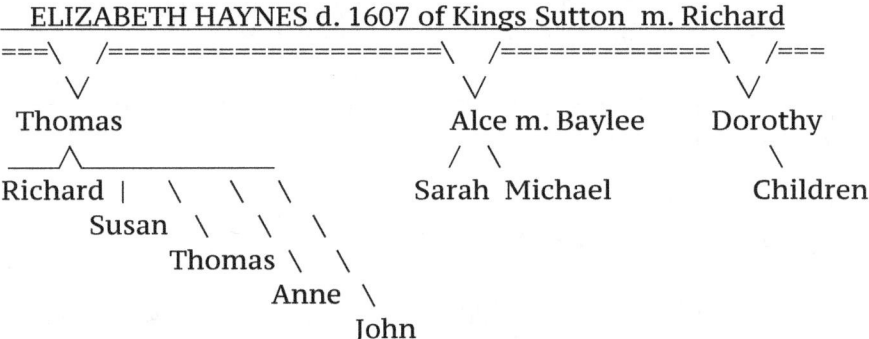

```
     ELIZABETH HAYNES d. 1607 of Kings Sutton  m. Richard
===\   /====================\   /============\   /===
    V                        V                V
  Thomas                 Alce m. Baylee    Dorothy
_____^_____        / \                \
Richard |  \  \  \     Sarah  Michael        Children
    Susan \   \  \
       Thomas \  \
          Anne \
             John
```

Whether this Elizabeth Haynes is connected to my Richard is unknown, even questionable, but I have a strong feeling that she is. In her will written 17 October 1606 and probated 18 January 1607, she mentioned only one son, Thomas, who had sons and daughters identical to the sons and daughters Marie Heynes mentioned in her will written twenty seven years later in 1633, and proved in 1634. Apparently this Thomas Heynes was Marie's husband and Elizabeth's only surviving son in 1606. The name of Elizabeth's deceased husband was probably Richard, as that is the name Marie Heynes, widow of Thomas and daughter-in-law of Elizabeth, had given their eldest son.

I have not yet found a will or any other provable evidence of the death of Elizabeth's husband, Richard, or Marie's husband, Thomas Heynes. I did find two burial notices in the Newbottle records, but they seem to be way too early. I suppose a Richard Heynes, son of Thomas of Kings Sutton, who was buried 11 Aug 1558 in Charlton/Newbottle Parish could have been Elizabeth's husband; but that is almost fifty years before Elizabeth died and it does seem unlikely. There is also a Thomas Heynes buried at Charleton/Newbottle on 21 April 1559, which seems unlikely as well. In these Newbottle records I also find "1509 Richard Haynes of Kings Sutton," mentioned. The records do not say who he is or what the event was. It does, however, establish an early Heynes/Haynes presence in Newbottle Parish where Richard and Margaret's first two children were baptized as well as a connection to Kings Sutton where Marie and her mother-in-law, Elizabeth, had both been living when they wrote their wills in 1606 and 1633.

My next important discovery was on microfilm #173603. It was a will probated in 1681 and written by John Haines of Kings Sutton in 1680, leaving property and money to, among others, his brother Richard of Banbury.

> *Amen 6th day of Nov 1680 Anno Domini, I <u>lohn Haines</u> of Kings Sutton in the county of Northamptonshire sick of body but of sound and perfect memory make this my last will and testament in the manner following. ... soul to God that gave it and my body in the earth whence it was taken. ... all that part of my messuage in Kings Sutton aforesaid which is free land and not held by copy of court roll and also all my airable land round lying and being in the fields of Kings Sutton aforesaid and in Astrope in the said county of Northampton which... copy of court roll with all and singular the appurtenances to the same belonging or in anywise ... and bequeath unto my <u>brother Richard Haines of Banbury</u> in the county of Oxon, yeoman, and my kinsman .Thomas Taylor, John Johnson, of Kings Sutton aforesaid and my kinsman and loving neighbor Henry Clement,. husbandman ... executors & admins. and assigns for the term of 7 years commencing from the day of my trust and confidence in them... that they and the survivors or survivor of them shall employ and lay.. the said pur... ... towards the payment of my just and due debts which I owe and the maintenance of my children. To my son Richard the sum of #30 of lawful money of England,*
>
> *Item: I give to my son Henry the sum of #20 of like lawful money*
>
> *Item: I give to my son Robert the sum of #20 and #5 of like lawful money,*
>
> *Item: I give to my son William the sum of #20 of like lawful money,*
>
> *Item: I give to my daughter Anne the sum of #20 of like ...,*
> *Item: I give to my daughter Judith the sum of #20 like and lawful money, ...and it is my willintent that the said legacies shall be paid by my son John, his heirs executors and administrators or assigns within 6...*

expiration of the said term of 7 years above mentioned and in case either any of my said children shall... by limited for payment of the said legacies then the legacy or legacies hereby given to him her or them ... to the survivor or survivors of them and in case my said son John shall make default in the ... of the said legacies at the time hereby limited for the payment thereof or in case any of my debts which then paid and sufficiently discharged then I devise give and bequeath all the said part of my messuage or land and not held by copy of court roll and all of my said airable land meadow, and greensward ground lying in Kings Sutton and Astrope aforesaid which is freeland and not held by copy of court rolls with all conditions whatsoever to the same belonging or... was appertaining to them my said <u>brother Richard Haines</u> and my kinsman Thomas Taylor and my kinsman john johnson and my neighbor Henry Clement and to their heirs and assigns forever upon the... in them. we repose that they the said Richard Haines, John Bricknell, John johnson and Henry Clement, the survivors and survivor of them shall be the sale of so much as shall be necessary to be sold out of the said land, money and thereof pay and discharge all my just and due debts which are secured by bond and then unpaid and all the legacies above... their sales of sufficient satisfaction for the case and pains and expense in the execution of the said trust and the ... which shall remain unsold... and over plus of the money shall remain and be conveyed to my said son lohn his ...

Item: After my debts are discharged I give and bequeath all the rest of my goods and chattels whatsoever to them John Bricknell, John Johnson and Henry Clement and I make them joint executors of this my last will and testament confident in the reposed that after my just and... debts are discharged they shall and will employ and layout the rest and remainder thereof for the maintenance of my said children and I revoke all former wills by me made and declare this to be my last will and testament.

In witness whereof I the said lohn Haines have hereunto set my hand and seal the day year first above written signed sealed and published in the presence of ... us ...

Thomas Taylor
Wm Dermond
Alexander Smith his mark
John Haines his mark
John Haynes of Kings Sutton

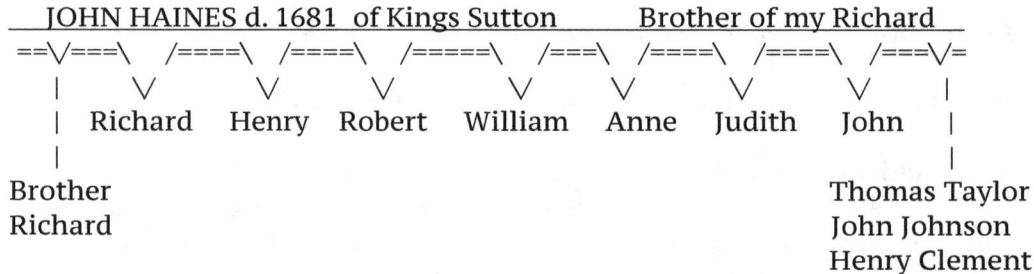

JOHN HAINES d. 1681 of Kings Sutton   Brother of my Richard

Richard   Henry   Robert   William   Anne   Judith   John

Brother   Thomas Taylor
Richard   John Johnson
                                             Henry Clement

This John Haynes must surely be the brother of my Richard, as my Richard definitely was a resident of Banbury at that time, and this will shows a definite family connection to Kings Sutton.   The village of Astrope, often called Easthorpe, mentioned in this will, is a large hamlet one mile east of Kings Sutton and west of Newbottle, and a member of both parishes.   Charlton, where Richard and Margaret were living when their children, Anna and John were born, is two thirds in Kings Sutton and one third in Newbottle Parish, near Aynhoe, about 4 miles southeast of Banbury.

John states right in his will that his brother Richard is "of Banbury" in 1680, just as John W. Haines has him there, and as I also have seen him mentioned in the Banbury Monthly Meeting records in that same time period.   Those particular Banbury Monthly Meeting records show my Richard signing Quaker marriage certificates every year from 1673 to 1681, and Margaret signing one in 1678.   The birth of their daughter, Mary in 1676, is also recorded in the Banbury Meeting records; all of which is ample evidence that my Richard and Margaret were definitely of Banbury in 1680 when John's will was written.

The bequest in 1681 of

> *all that part of my messuage in Kings Sutton aforesaid which is free land and not held by copy of court roll and also all of my airable land round lying and being in the fields of Kings Sutton and in Astrope in the said county of Northampton which...copy of court roll with all and singular the appurtenances to the same belonging or in any wise...bequeath unto my brother Richard Haines of Banbury in the county of Oxon, yeoman*

and others from his brother John would certainly have provided the wherewithal for my Richard to buy property in America and emigrate in 1682.

This John Haines of Kings Sutton was probably not Marie's son, John. Marie's son would have been at least 73 years of age, and probably older in 1680. And that would mean his brother, my Richard of Banbury, would also have been too old to emigrate and have young children since he was also mentioned 73 years earlier in that same will.   But this John Haines could very well have been Marie's grandson. I have yet to find, however, any evidence of birth, marriage or children's baptisms for Marie's son John Heynes.

More Astounding Discoveries 4

I looked again for a marriage of Richard Haines and Margaret ca1659 and 1660 in Newbottle Parish where their children, Anna and Johannes, were baptized. but again, found only:

Anno Dom: 1660
Nulla Nuptia hoc anno celebrate

I searched in every other nearby parish where Margaret might have been born, where they might have married by banns. I could not find a marriage in the late 1650's or early 1660's of any Richard Haines and Margaret occurring at any appropriate time and place to be my Richard and Margaret. I searched for the marriage of Thomas Heyns and Marie Pargiter. Marie had mentioned her brothers John and Thomas Pargiter in her will, thus proving her maiden name. I found no marriage for Marie Pargiter and Thomas Heynes, but I did find a John Pargiter born to John Pargiter of Astrop on 13 May 1651 in the Newbottle records, the same records that held the birth of Richard and Margaret's first two children. In these Newbottle records there was also a Richard Haynes/Heynes baptized in 1558 who could have been the husband of Elizabeth who died in 1607. I did find Marie (Pargiter) Heynes's birth and her parents' marriage in the *Aynho Parish Register, 1562-1709,* the same records that held the baptisms of three of my Richard and Margaret's sons.

Marie's parents, Robert Pargiter and Katharina Yate were married 15 Oct 1582, and Marie was baptized 17 Sep 1583. Marie was baptized at Aynhoe, so her marriage to Thomas should have been there also. But it was not to be found in the readable portions of these parish records. I went through those records again in January, 2014, examining every line on every page, hoping to find and record any and all Haines, Haynes, Heynes, Hands, etc. baptisms, marriages and burials which might be there recorded. I found a Rudolphus Handes filia Roberti baptized 7 December 1584, but not another Haines of any spelling until 6 Aug 1665, when my ancestor, Richard Heyns son of Richard and Margaret appeared. Then on the page dated 22 December, 1666, I found "*Thomas Heyn son of Richard and Margaret*", and on 24 April 1672, "*William son of Rich and Marg. Hains*", both sons of my Richard. The next Haynes listed was on 13 March 1686, and it was "Anne daughter of Thomas et Elizabeth Haynes," certainly not my family. Then on 25 March 1690, there was an "*Elizabeth daughter of Thomas and Elizabeth Haynes;"* and on 31 Jul 1698 a *"Benjamin, son of Thomas and Margaret Heynes of Kings Sutton."* These were also much too late to be closely connected to my Richard. The marriage records begin in 1573, and on 14 October 1581 *"Jacobus Parker de Aynoe et Janum Heynes"* were married. Pages were missing from the book for the years 1589 through 1591; but in 1592, on "2 February Richardus Haynes de Aynhoe married Annam Farman de Sutton". This Richard and Anne could possibly have been the right age to be parents of John Haynes who died in 1680, but more likely the right age to be his grandparents. There were no marriages listed between 26 Mar 1659 and 1 July 1665 in this book. After the page beginning DEATHS AND BURIALS anno Domini 1570 I found the following listed.

Feb 1573 Robertus Heynes de Aynhoe
14 Feb 1584 Joha Haynes de Aynhoe vidua.

From 1643 to 1652 there are only sporadic entries, very dim and mostly illegible, but, since their first child was born in 1661 my Richard and Margaret's marriage would probably not have taken place during those years. The Marriage records of Kings Sutton contained several Haynes's, but only one of interest. A John Haynes who married in 1643, but with no other identifying information. The Kings Sutton Marriages also contained five Heynes's: Alice who married in 1582, Anna in 1577, Elizabeth in 1598, Richard in 1589, and Thomas in 1601. At first I thought they could all be the children or grandchildren of Elizabeth Heynes who died in 1607 at Kings Sutton. But then on another page, the names of both bride and groom are mentioned, none of which are mine except Alexander Smith and Agneta Haines who married 22 May 1610. In old English records the names Anna and Agnes were sometimes interchangeable. Agneta is the Latin form of Agnes, and this Agneta is probably the grand daughter of Thomas Heynes mentioned in the 1633 will of his widow, Marie (Pargiter) Heynes. Since these records also contain the baptisms of my Richard and Margaret Haines' three sons, albeit fifty years later, I believe it does hint strongly at a connection between Marie's family and my Richard.

I searched for a marriage of any Richard Heynes and Elizabeth sometime in the 1500's, hoping to identify the husband of Elizabeth who died in 1607. I found only one: a 1581 marriage of Richard Heynes and Elizabeth Palmer in Swerford, Oxfordshire County. *"Swerford is a small village on the river Swere south of Hook Norton and north of Little Tew and to the northwest of the town of Chipping Norton."* It's about nine miles southwest of Kings Sutton. This could have been Elizabeth (d. 1607), and her husband, Richard; since by the time she died they would have been married 25 years.

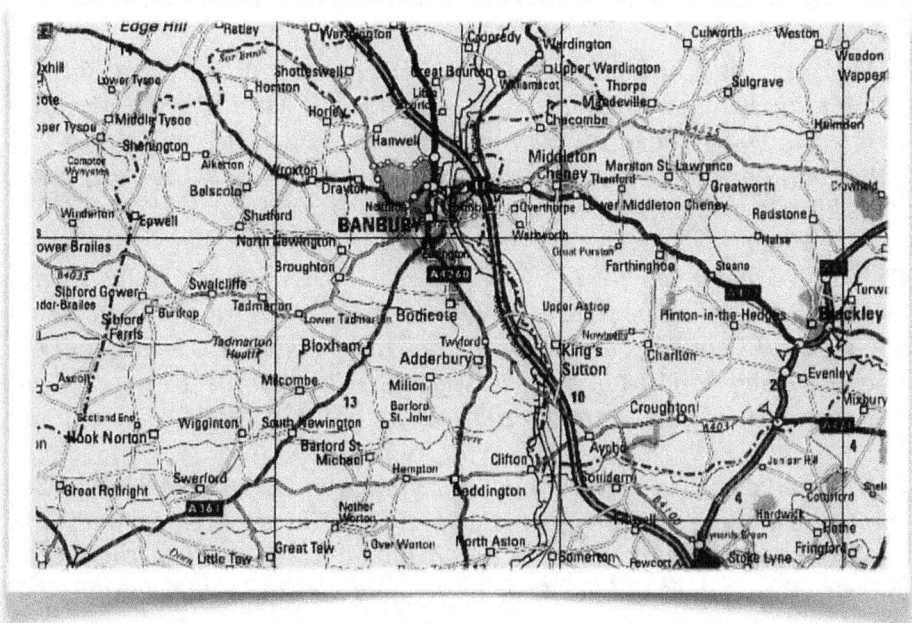

Finding this marriage moved my research area to Oxfordshire County where I found on microfilm *#95063, British Court Records,* many Heynes's, although none who fit the requirements of my proven ancestors until I happened onto one more old will that contained words which caught my attention, words that again made me think Swerford and Kings Sutton may be connected.

> *Testament of JOHANNES HAYNES of Swarford, Oxon, yeoman.   In The Name of God Amen, the tenth day of September anno Domini 1607 the (fifth or first) year of the reign of our sovereign Lord James by the grace of god of England France and Ireland, King and defender of the faith. and of his reign of Scotland ye XLI th (41st)   I JOHN Haynes of Swerford in the county of Oxford, yeoman, being sick of body but of perfect remembrance thanks to Almighty God do make and declare this my last will and testament in manner and form following:*
>
> *First and chiefly I give and commend my soul into the hands of almighty God and my body to be buried in the church of Swarford aforesaid. Perfect worldly wealth, as it hath pleased God to bestow upon me I give and bequeath as followeth:*
>
> *First I give to the mother church of Oxford VI (money). For my land in warwick here my will and meaning and I give and bequeath to my eldest son RICHARD Haines all these my tenement and lands lying and being in Henley*

in Arden. And whether and fields hereof within the said county of Warr. (Warwick) and further I give unto him 6 pounds 13 shillings and three pense in money to be paid unto him by my executors at the age of XV (15) years to be disposed for him and to his use by the discretion of my overseers.

ITEM: I give and bequeath to EDWARD Haines my youngest son these lands of mine lying and being in --- of --- Knoll within the said county of Warrick commonly called by the name of Flaxbutts Field and also 6 lbs 13 shillings in money to be paid to him at the age of 15 years to be disposed for him for his use by the discretion of my overseers.

ITEM: I give and bequeath to my second son JOHN Haines 20 lbs in money wherof my will is shall be paid unto him by my executor at the age also of 15 years, six lbs 13 shillings and 3 or 4 pence to be disposed for him and to his use by the discretion of my overseers. and be the residue 13 lbs 6 shillings and 8 pence to be paid unto him the said John at the age of 21 years.

ITEM: I give and bequeath to my eldest daughter SUSANNA Haines 20 lbs in money. To my second daughter ELIZABETH Haynes 20 lbs money and to my youngest daughter EDITH 20 lbs in money to be paid to them also at theyr age of --- days of the age of 15 years or else at their days of marriage when it shall happen --- months space next after the said days or marriage provided and my will and meaning is that if any of my foresaid children should happen to decease before the time herein appointed for the payment and receiving of their portions before named so that then the person or legacy of him or her so deceasing shall be equally divided and receive to the residue --- by both sons and daughters. Also I give and bequeath to my sister ALICE, her two children either of them one ewe sheep of five shillings price apeace at the discretion of my overseers. Also I give to my MOTHER forty shillings of money the residue of my goods whatsoever after the performance of this my will and payment of my debts. I bequeath and leave to my wyffe PHILLIPP Haines whosoever I make and appoint sole executor of this my last will and testament. Also I do make choice of and appoint my brother Richard Haynes and Anthony Lizzard to be my overseers for the better [per]formance hereof.

I have hereunto put my hand the day and year 1st above written in the presence of these --- named by me John Haynes.

Witnesses: Richard Haynes, Anthony Heywood, Rich. Channey, Geo. Heynes

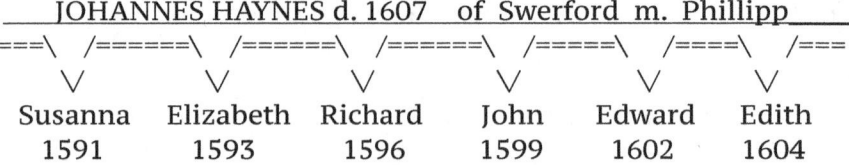

The words that caught my attention were: "*my sister Alce, her two children*". This John Heynes, who I will hereafter refer to as John/1, wrote his will 10 September 1607 and he was buried thirteen days later on 23 September. He gave his mother 40 shillings, mentioned daughters Susannah, Elizabeth, and Edith, a brother Richard Heynes and his "*sister Alce, her two children*", while Elizabeth, in her 17 Oct 1606 will, gave money to "...*my daughter Alce her son*," and "...*daughter to my daughter Alce*". These two children of "*my sister Alce*" and "*my daughter Alce*" lead me to believe that John/1 might be the son of Elizabeth who died in 1607 and brother to her daughter, Alce.

At first I thought, "*No.*" "*It can't be.*" John/1 was buried 23 September, 1607, eleven months after Elizabeth wrote her will on 17 Oct 1606, and she died sometime before 18 January 1607 when her will was proved. She would not have been alive to receive the money when he died, or even when his will was written on 10 September. But then I remembered. Using the old style calendar, which was in effect until 1752, the year begins 25 March, not 1 January. Therefore September came before January in 1607, and John/1 died four months before Elizabeth. She would definitely have been alive to receive the 40 shillings.

This was all very interesting and did seem like it should relate to my family somehow; but all I had to go on was a hunch, a very strong feeling that these two were connected to my Richard in some way. But I had no evidence to show Elizabeth having any connection with John/1 other than their common surnames, albeit with different spellings, and the meaning of those words which caught my eye in both wills.

Every genealogist knows not to ignore the value of a hunch; but there were other questionable considerations. Location and family. John was buried in the church at Swerford and Elizabeth was buried in the churchyard at Kings Sutton, about nine miles distant. No connection there. And while Elizabeth makes no mention of a son, Richard, in her will; John/1 does name a brother, Richard, in his. Maybe my hunch was wrong. Maybe I was jumping to conclusions, seeing what I wanted to see rather than what really was. But being unwilling to give up so easily, and wanting so badly for them to be related, I re-examined the facts I already knew to be accurate. Since I had seen that marriage of Richard Haines and Elizabeth Palmer as well as John/1's will in Swerford, I went back to the Swerford indexes hoping to find some other clue. And sure enough, there it was. I found a transcript of the *Swerford Parish Records on fiche #6142087.*

The first page of the transcript tells me that the original parish register was transcribed and typed by Mrs. N. Clifton, Senendone House, Shennington, and indexed in the Oxfordshire History Centre in July 1986. It states that the first register contains some baptisms from 1577 to 1633, some marriages from 1579 to 1633, and some burials from 1578 to 1633 as well as some out-of-sequence entries. The second register contains some baptisms from 1633-1745, some burials from 1633 to 1745, and some marriages from 1633 to 1745. The transcript is badly typed, very mixed up, and I thought it may not be complete. Several of the family's marriages and burials are missing, but it does contain the births of children John/1 mentions in his will, as well as his own burial on 23 Sep 1607.

In July, 2013, after writing to the Oxfordshire History Centre in England where old records are held, I traveled there to see the records for myself.

The Enquiry Desk and the reading room at the Oxfordshire History Centre.

I wanted to know if the transcripts I had were as complete and accurate as can be found at the present time. I knew I would only be satisfied upon personal examination. And I did have a personal examination. At the Oxfordshire History Centre the original sixteenth century record books came to me resting on a pillow. I was given permission to photograph the ancient pages, although use of any flash was prohibited. After being directed to a table where the light was best for photography, I was given three small round black leather weights to hold the books open, and a pair of dingy and well worn white cotton gloves to wear while handling these delicate old pages

The books appeared to be very old. One was covered in black leather, very worn, cracked and tattered. The spine appeared to have a standard binding, and it had metal clasps to hold it closed. The other, which looked newer, but later proved to contain the oldest records, was covered in a light beige, almost a cream-colored leather. It had two small squares of what appeared to be the same leather, hand stitched to the spine for reinforcement, with strings of the same animal hide used to tie it closed.

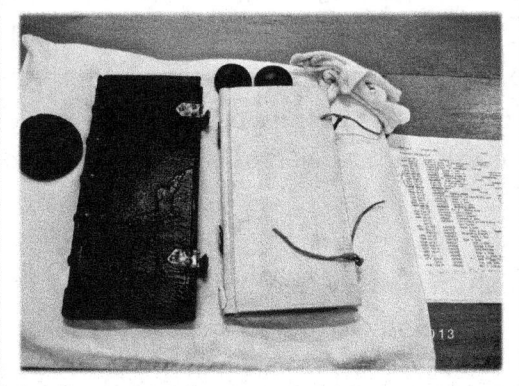

Original 1577-1675 Swerford Parish record books

There were many worn parts within the earliest years pages in these old original records, and parts of some pages appeared to have been preserved by some type of lamination-like reinforcement. This gave them some stability, and I perused every page, even photographed some. Notice the worn and repaired paper on the upper left corner of the page in this picture of 1599 records shown on the left. The birth register of John Hannes is the third line from the bottom of the page.

I did finally have satisfaction. The information in these original records, the Haines, Haynes, Hanns, Hannes, Heines, Heynes entries which I have inserted here with my presumed family members in bold print, and pictures of original records, was exactly the same as the transcripts I had been working with in Salt Lake City.

HAINES, HAYNES, HANNS, HANNES, HEINES, HEYNES,

Marriages, Chrystenings and Burials synce the years of our Lorde God 1577 of Swerford Parish, Oxfordshire, England

1581 Oct 27 Geo HANNES baptized

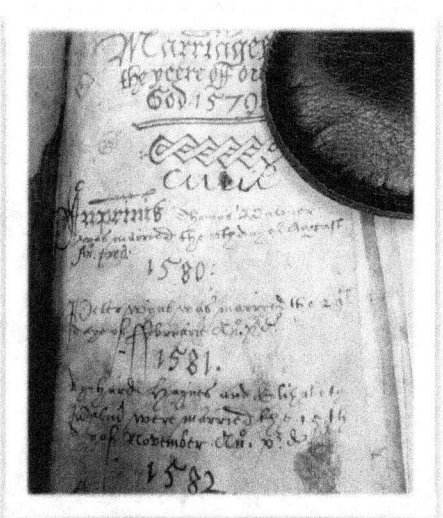

1581, Nov 15 Rchd. HAYNES & Elizabeth PALM(ER) married

1582 May 31   EIDES, Henrye & HAYNES, Eliz., wid.   married
1582, Oct 25 Anthony HAINES buried
1583 Jun 5 John HEYNES burie

1585, 86, (missing), 1587 Apr 15 Rychard HANNES baptized

1589 Sept 13 BROWNE, John & HANES, Agnes   married
  "   Feb 23   HEYNES, Agnes, wid.   buried
1590 Jan 28   HAWKYNS, John & HANNS,Eliz.   married

1591, Mar 27, Susan HAN(N)ES, daughter of John was baptized

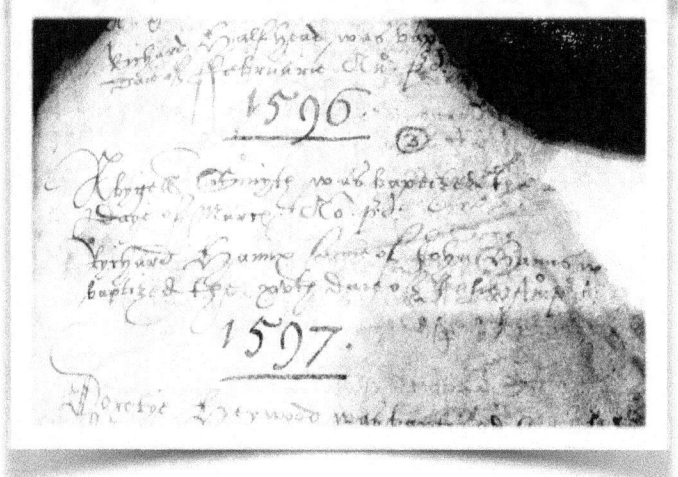

1596 July 15   Richd HANNES son of John was baptized

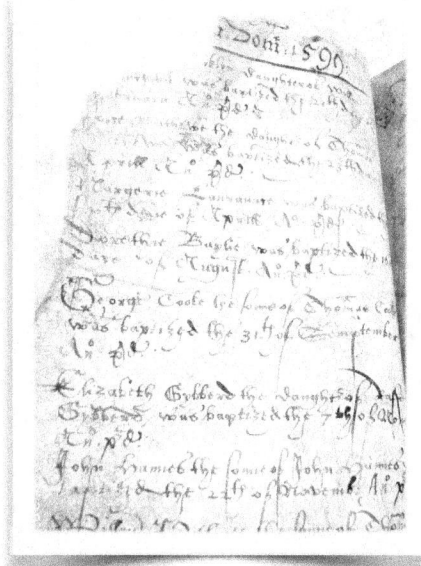

John HANNES the sonne of John HANNES was baptized the 22 day of November 1599

1602   Mar 26   HAYNES als.Radford, Rchd.   buried

38

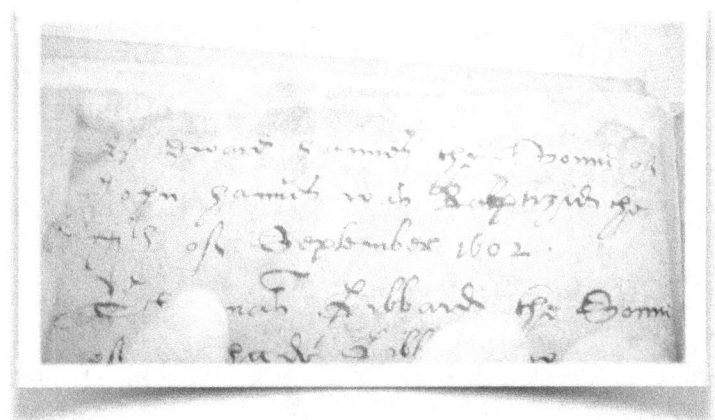

Edward HANNES the sonne of John HANNES was baptized the 11th day of September 1602.

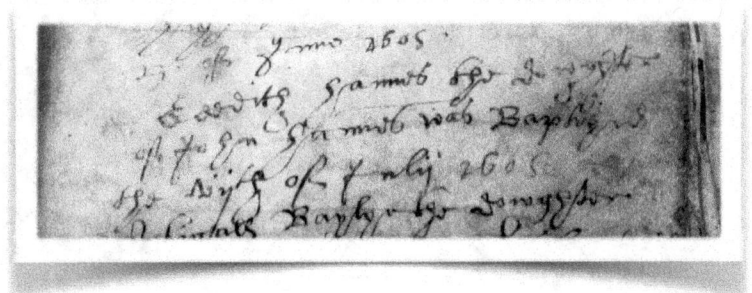

1605 July 7 Eeedith(sic) HANNES, the daughter of John Hannes was baptized

1607 John HANNES was buried the 23 day of September

1617 Jul 30 HEINES, Geo.buried

1625 John HANNES the sonne of John H A N N E S w a s baptized 2 Oct

1625 Nov 21 HEINES als Radford, Thos & L A W R E N C E , J a n e married

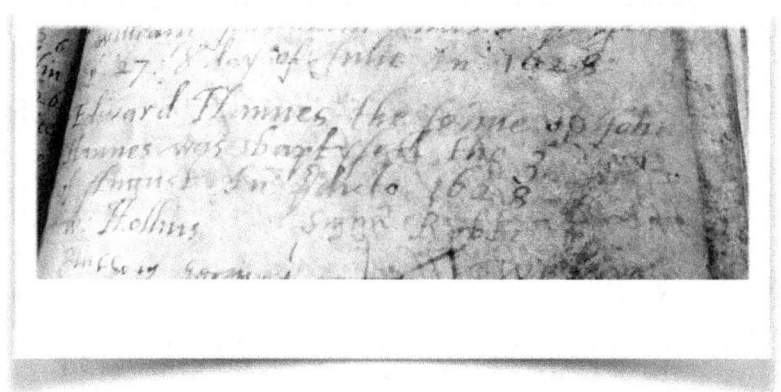

1628 Aug 3 EDWARD HANNES sonne of JOHN HANNES baptized

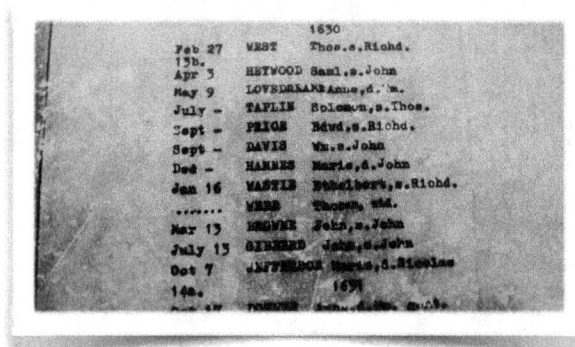

1630 Dec ? HANNES, Marie, d. John   baptized
(Photo of the records transcript at Salt Lake City)

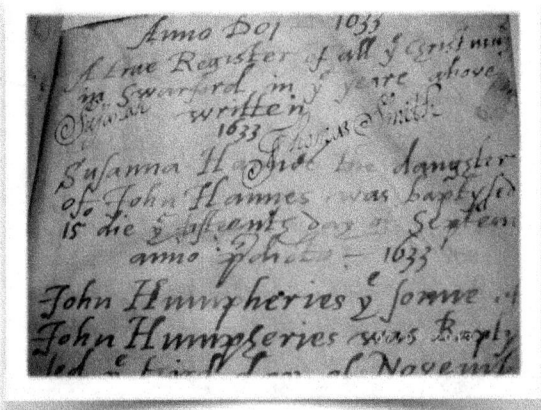

1633   Sept 15 , Susanna HANNES the daughter of John Hannes was baptized

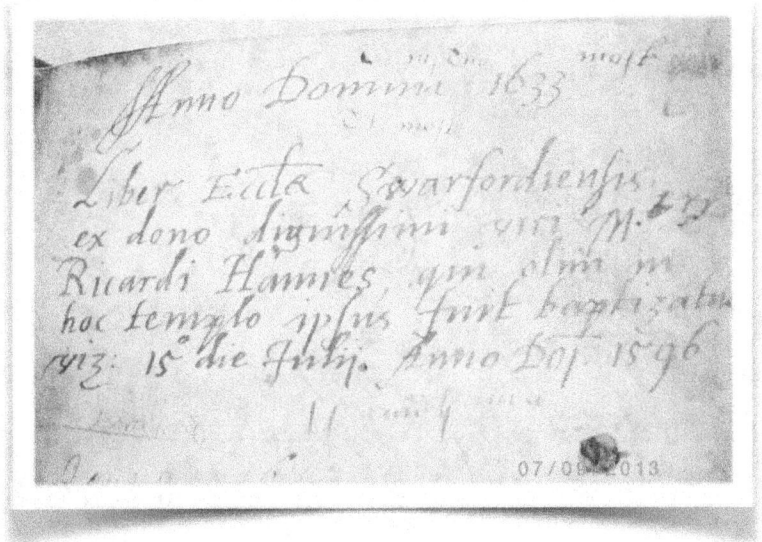

What is this - - Liber Ecta?

This 1633 entry was the only item on this page in the older-looking dark-covered book, and it was on one of the first pages of that book. It was a mystery. Obviously not a baptism, burial, or marriage record. It was also obvious that this Ricardi Hannes was John/1's eldest son, the one who inherited property at Henley in Arden. I wondered what the meaning is of this Latin writing in these Swerford Parish Records. Why was Richard mentioned here? Liber? Something about books? In January, 2015 I was fortunate to find a helper at the Family History Library in Salt Lake City who could help me translate. It appears to be a notation stating that the book was presented to the parish by Mr. Richard Hannes, a man of great dignity and wealth who himself was baptized in the Swerford Church on 15 July 1596. The helper also told me that one pound at that time was equal to about 10,000 dollars in today's money. John/1's request to be buried in the church had already apprised me of the fact that the family was wealthy, but nevertheless, I was pleased to discover evidence of this generous gift by his eldest son.

1635 Richard HANNES the sonne of John Hannes was baptized the 20 day of March

1635 Nov 12 E d w a r d HANNES, & Medes, Anne married

1636 Aug 14 John HANNES son of Edward Hannes was baptized

1637 Feb 4 Edith HANNES daughter of Edward baptized

1640 Jan 10 William HANNES & Richard Hannes the son's of Edward Hannes and Ane his wife were baptized

1640 Jan 14 William Hannes son of Edw. & Anne buried

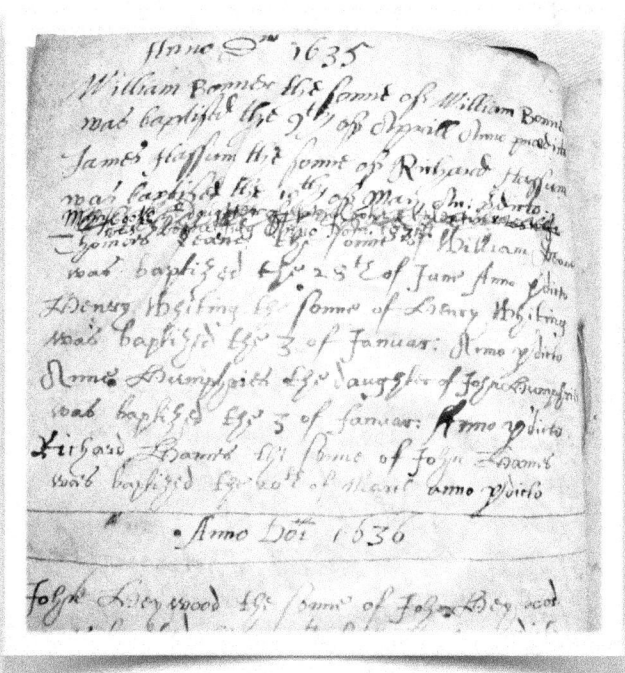

1640 Jun 22 Elizabeth HANNS the daughter of John Hannes was baptized

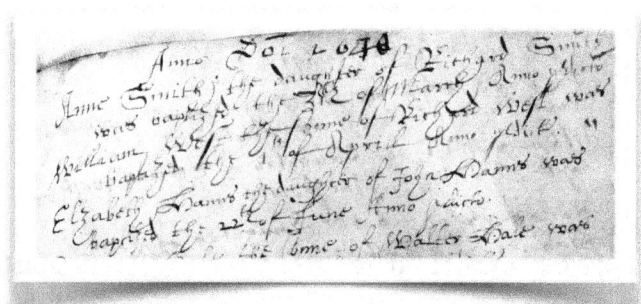

1641 Jun 16 SARAH HANNES the daughter of JOHN Hannes baptized

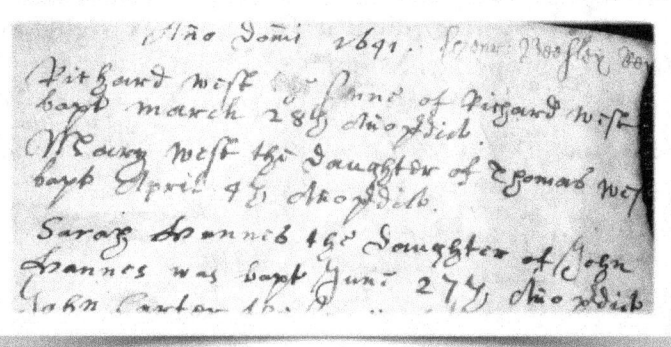

1642	May 17	HAINES	Thos. s. Geo.	baptized
"	May 24	HAINES	Thos. s. Geo.	buried
1642	Sept 25	Elizabeth HANNES dau. of Edward		baptized
1643	Jun 22	HAINES	Richd. s. Geo. baptized	24 Jun
1644	Jun 11	HANNES	Edw. s. Edw.	baptized
1646	Jul 3	William	HANNS son of Edw Hannes.	
1648	Dec	RICHARD HANNS Cottager		was buried
1650	May 7	HANNS	Martha d. Edw.	baptized
1657	Nov 9	HANNS	John the Elder	buried
1663	Nov 7	HANNS	Edw. s. Edw.	buried
1666		HANNS	Rchd. s. John	died at Barford
1674	Jun 23	HANNS	Edw. (age) 72 yrs	.buried
"	Oct 3	HANNS	Ann wid. Edw.	buried

I went through the transcript line by line from the beginning in 1577 to the 1680's. I separated out all the Hannes, Hanns, Haines, and Heynes's, and listed the marriages, births and burials separately and chronologically. I was able to combine this list with the names of John/1's daughters Susan, Elizabeth and Edith along with sons, John, Richard and Edward in his 1607 will to make a feasible pedigree outline which clearly shows the possibility for this to be the family of my Richard.

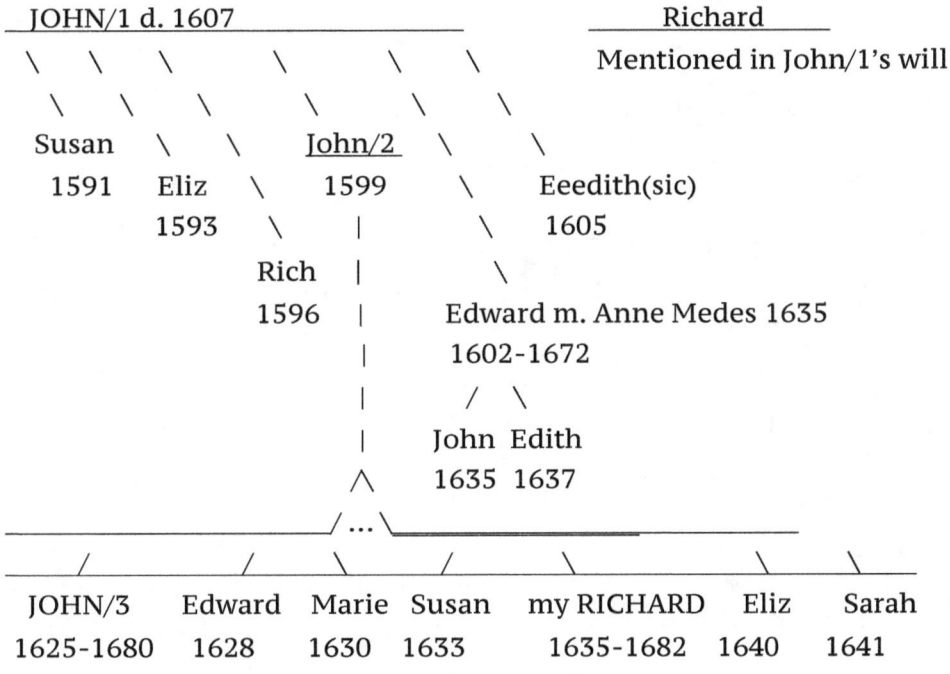

Also noted is the fact that each and every one of these entries that fit my family is spelled either HANNES or HANNS in the original records except for the marriage of Richard HAYNES and Elizabeth Palmer. There was also a Rychard Hannes chrystened in what appears to be 1587. He could possibly be another son of John, or even a brother; but the father's name is not mentioned in this record as it is with all his other children. And unless he died young, this Rychard is probably not the son of John/1, as John/1 says in his will that his eldest son is Richard, the "Ricd. s. John chrystened" in 1596 as it is listed in the parish records. This Rychard, born 1587 would have been twenty years old in 1607 when John/1 wrote his will. He might have been the brother, Richard, that John/1 had appointed to be one of the overseers of his will.

I found a lack of information in these parish records where some marriages and burials should have been entered. The burial of Edward's mother, heiress to property at Knowle, sometime after Edward's birth in 1602 was missing. Also missing were the marriage dates of John/1 to his first wife, whose name I believe may have been Marie or Edith, and to Phillipp, the wife he named executrix in his will. I learned later that a marriage by banns always took place at the home of the bride, but a marriage by license could take place anywhere. Was there more information somewhere else?

By this time in my research, I had learned something about old English traditions, and I now believe that since John/1 bequeathed property at Henley in Arden to his eldest son, he either inherited or was given that property; indicating that he may have been born there.   But he also left property at Knowle to his youngest son while leaving only money to his second son. Apparently this division of assets was appropriate, as T. W. Downing lists the Customs of The Manor by item-number in his 1914 collection of *The Records of Knowle,* and on page 409, the 14th Item states

> *that if any Man Marry a Woman that is an Heir to any Copyhold Land within this Mannor and she die before her Husband, then the first Husband of the sd Woman must of right have all his Wife's Land as his Free bench. And after his Decease the youngest Son and for want of a Son the Youngest Daughter of the sd Woman by the first Husband must inherit the Mother's Land.*

I believe John/1 was married first in 1589 or 1590 because the baptism of his first daughter, Susannah, was registered in 1591, at Swerford Parish in Oxfordshire as were all the rest of his children baptized at Swerford. I believe his first marriage took place at Knowle in Warwickshire because marriages were usually performed at the home of the bride, and because he bequeathed property at Knowle to his youngest son, Edward, who was born in 1602. He apparently had come by this property at Knowle through his marriage to Edward's mother. But, as all his children and even his own burial were recorded in the Swerford Parish Records in Oxfordshire, he obviously did not live on this property at Knowle in Warwickshire. And neither did his youngest son, Edward, who had inherited that property.   Edward stayed at Swerford where he married Anne Medes on 12 November 1635, and fathered six children, before his death at Swerford in 1672.

I have no information about Edward's mother, but according to the Swerford Parish Records and the naming patterns of the time, her given name may have been Edith, as that was the name Edward gave his first daughter. Or, he may have given his daughter that name to honor his younger sister, Eeedith(sic), who was born 7 Jul 1605. His mother's name may have been Edith, but I think it was more likely Marie, since that is the name Edward's older brother, John, born 1599, gave his first daughter. This, of course, unless Richard had a different mother. I have found no records for the death of an Edith or a Marie Hannes between 1602 when Edward was born or around 1605 when Edith was born, appropriate times before John/1 might have married Phillipp.

Looking again at John/1's will, his bequest of land and property at Henley in Arden tells me that he came from Warwickshire, that he was probably an eldest son with inherited property, and that he left that property to his eldest son, Richard, just as England's law of primogeniture dictates. So I wrote the Warwickshire Public Record Office for evidence of John's birth in about 1565 or 70 at Henley in Arden and/or his marriage in about 1589 or 90 at Knowle, in Warwickshire. The Archivist at the Record Office answered my questions with:

> *In regards to property held in Henley in Arden, it is normal for there to be no records surviving....I checked for deeds relating to Henley in Arden,...there are some surviving from that early....(one) mentions a party named John Heynes of Henley in Arden, baker as one of 16 parties in an indenture regarding the uses of land in various parishes including Henley in Arden. This attested copy is dated 10th May 1680 which is too late for your John Heynes and I could find no indication of whether the indenture was copied from an earlier deed. You are welcome to view the document but it may not be relative.*

That settled the question of finding a record of John/1's birth, and as to my query about a marriage record, the answer was:

> *Unfortunately the earliest surviving parish registers for Knowle are from 1682 onwards, including marriage registers, therefore there is unlikely to be a record of a marriage in 1591. We hold parish registers of baptisms, marriages and burials for Warwickshire here, including Henley in Arden and Knowle; these are available to view on microfilm in our search room but are also available on www.ancestry.co.uk. On this website our databases are most easily accessed by choosing the 'Card Catalog' option under the 'Search' menu and then searching in the title box for Warwickshire.*

I did go on ancestry.co.uk and although there is a multitude of Haines, Hanes, Hannes, Haynes, Heins, or Heynes marriages, baptisms, and burials, found none that seemed to be dated at the right time and place to be my ancestor.

The abundance of documentary facts and details gleaned from these parish records and old wills opens the door to several relationship possibilities which so far, lack any documentary evidence, but which seem plausible to me.

John/1's middle son, John/2, who was born in 1599, named his first daughter Marie and his second daughter Susan. That fits with my idea that John/1's father, who I think was a Richard, possibly married a Susan first. Then Susan would have been John/1's mother and Marie would have been his wife, the mother of his children. Marie would have been the heiress of Knowle, and Edward might have named his first daughter for his sister, Edith, as I said previously. Or his first wife, Marie, may have died, leaving John/1 free to marry Edith, heiress of Knowle. Or, this Edith may have been the mother of John/1's youngest daughter, Edith, as well as his youngest son, Edward. This record is missing.

Or Phillipp could be mother to Edith. She may have been heiress to a tenancy at Swerford, and if so, John/1 would have had free bench to that tenancy until he died, just as he had had free bench to the tenancy at Knowle in Warwickshire. At his death it would have gone back to Phllipp's youngest child if she had any children. It apparently did go back to Phillipp if it was hers, as John/1 gives only money to his middle son and his daughters. He does not mention Swerford property at all in his will. He says only that

> the residue of my goods whatsoever after the performance of this my will and payment of my debts I bequeath and leave to my wyffe Phillipp Haines whosoever I make and appoint sole executor of this my last will and testament.

Perhaps Edward did name his first daughter for his younger sister who was born 7 July 1605. Perhaps naming patterns are not always followed religiously.

If John/1's mother was a Susan or Susanna, it would validate the possibility that the Richard Haines and Elizabeth Palmer, who were married at Swerford in 1581, could have been his father and stepmother. Elizabeth did not have to be Richard's first wife to fit the family pattern. I am now considering the possibility that John/1 and Thomas, husband of Marie Heynes who died in 1634, are brothers who may have been sons of an unknown first wife, Susan or Susanna. And the rest of the children may have been Elizabeth's as shown in the chart following. But I have yet to find evidence of such a marriage.

Italic print in the following chart indicates fact from either a will or parish record. All else is my assumption, including some of their places in the family.

47

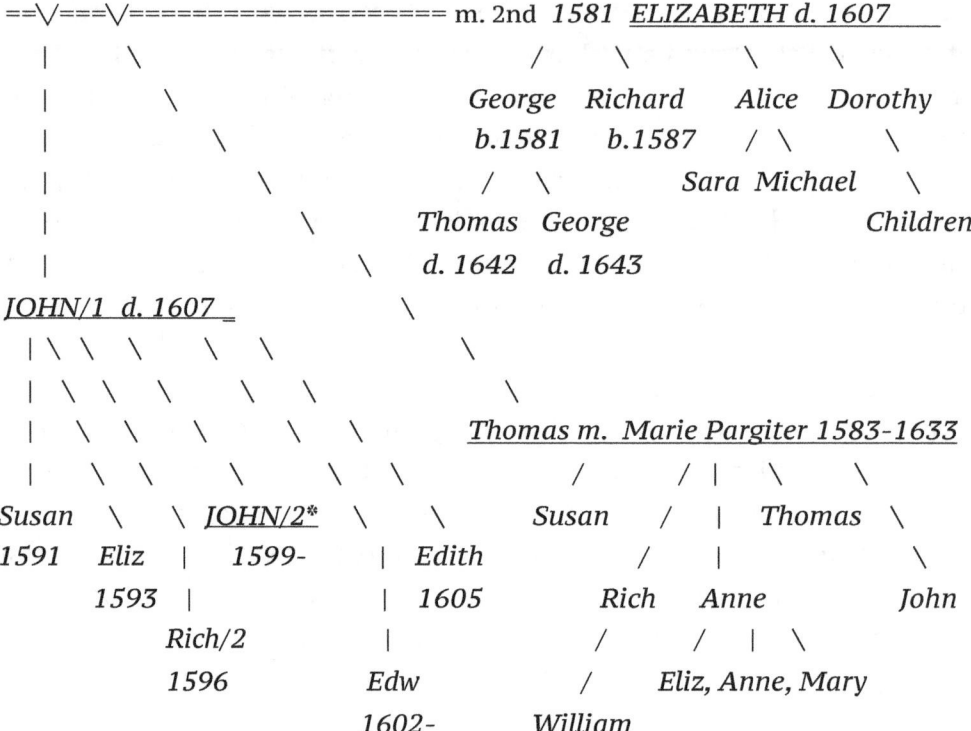

RICHARD/1 *of Henley in Arden* m. ca 1565 SUSAN?
==∨===∨==================== m. 2nd *1581 ELIZABETH d. 1607*

George	Richard	Alice	Dorothy
b.1581	b.1587	/ \	\
		Sara Michael	\
Thomas	George		Children
d. 1642	d. 1643		

JOHN/1 *d. 1607*

Thomas m. *Marie Pargiter 1583-1633*

Susan			JOHN/2*			Susan		Thomas	
1591	Eliz		1599-	Edith					
	1593			1605		Rich	Anne		John
	Rich/2					/	/ \	
	1596		Edw				Eliz, Anne, Mary	
			1602-	William				

The Records of Knowle, previously mentioned, was full of wonderful information, most of which, I discovered while scouring it's contents, is about people who lived there long after my family. But it did verify a connection to John/1 on page 391. Within a list of

> *gent. and others, of the value and yearly rents of their lands lying in the constabulary of Knoll who are not there residinge*

for Poll Tax in 1660 is

> *Edward Hannes, of _____, yeoman, in Northamptonshire, 005 pounds - 00 - shillings - 00 pence.*

This surely must be Edward, the youngest son of John/1, who had been bequeathed the said property at Knowle and was "not there residinge" in 1660. But he was required to pay a poll tax. It shows that Edward had copyhold land at Knowle but definitely had him residing in Northamptonshire in 1660 rather than Knowle in Warwickshire, where he had property, or Swerford in Oxfordshire where he was baptized. Kings Sutton is located in Northamptonshire, and if Edward was in Northamptonshire in 1660, his older brother John/2, born 1599, may also have been living there. John/2 might have used the inheritance of twenty pounds that he was to have received at his age of twenty-one, which occurred in 1620, (see will of John/1, pp. 31-32) to buy property in and around Kings Sutton. I believe that this John/2 was the father of John Haines who died in 1680, the John Haines who left property in Kings Sutton to his brother, Richard Haines, my known ancestor who died at sea in 1682.

Also in this old book, on page 383 and 384, I find the names

Thomas Heanes, weaver, and Mary his wife, 0 - 1 - 0,

and

John Heanes, weaver, his sonne,   *0 - 1 - 0,*

both living at Knowle at the time of the 1660 poll tax, and both probably related to John/1 in some way. It also verifies that some Heynes descendants continued living in Warwickshire for many more years. On page 7 of *The Records of Knowle* within a list of 1685 marriages and burials is noted:

Bur. Thomas Heynes was buryd the twenty fift day of July.

And on page 65 a 1693 marriage of

Joseph Lawrence and Anne Heynes both of Rowington the 4th of November.

I did find two more old books with several Hannes, etc., listed in the contents. The Introduction of *The Register of the Guild of Knowle in the County of Warwick, 1451-1535: From the Original..by William B. Bickley.* states that a 15th century Guild was

an association of persons banded together for mutual aid, benefit, and protection. Guilds varied greatly as to importance and number of members, from small craft guilds composed of a few tradesmen of similar branches of a similar trade to popular religious and social guilds which could boast of several thousand members enlisted from every class of society, irrespective of trade or occupation

The objects of guilds varied but little, and included chiefly religious worship; aid in sickness, old age, poverty, losses by fire, water, shipwreck, or wrongful imprisonment; the visitation of prisoners, and provision of work; the contributing to all kinds of charitable work, and towards the founding and maintenance of churches, schools, bridges, town walls, &c; supplying loans to deserving members; burying the dead with suitable religious rites;

condoling with mourners, and providing masses and prayers for the souls of departed members.

Guilds also regularly held social and business meetings, and periodical feasts; occasionally providing minstrels and players; and undertook the performance of miracle plays, processions and pageants...

There is little doubt that their chief and direct objects were to encourage charity, and useful living: members were admitted upon payment of entrance fees, and taking oaths to observe the rules, and the expenses were supported by donations and annual subscriptions, though many guilds had besides, lands and possessions, which had from time to time been bequeathed to them...p.x,ix

Bickley also says that *"The Guild of Knowle, for the most part, seems to have been composed of the ordinary people of Warwickshire and districts adjoining". p.xiv* And that persons could be members of more than one guild. The Guild of Knowle was apparently a religious guild as the register mentions the existence of a Chapel at Knowle in the 13th century, and "praying for the soul of a loved one" seems to be the purpose of many of the persons listed. Vivian Bird, who wrote *A SHORT HISTORY OF WARWICKSHIRE AND BIRMINGHAM,* validates this assumption when he writes

the fundamental object of some gilds was to ensure the salvation after death of the souls of its members,(as well as) to supervise members conduct, and adjudicate in disputes between them so that they did not have recourse to law.

He also said that

membership in a gild was open to all who qualified by business, trade, and status...Admittance fees ranged from 20 pence to 20 shillings plus a levy for keeping lighted candles on the alter of the Gild Chapel, though some members were enrolled gratis on their promise to perform work for the gild,

and that

Knowle's Gild, in addition to all the great Warwickshire families, enrolled national figures including the second Marquis of Dorset, grandfather of Lady Jane Grey, and Henry VII's hated Chancellor, Sir Richard Empson, a ruthless servant of an avaricious monarch. When Henry VIII dissolved it the Gild of Knowle owned land as far distant as Halesowen and London. Today (1977) the old Gild House still stands beside Knowle Church.

A large variety of different and geographically widespread Parishes are mentioned as places of residence by members listed in the *Register of the Guild of Knowle.* Some with possible connections to my Haines line, such as "Robertus pgitur(Pargiter) de gritworth"(Greatworth) in 1514 and a Thomas pgetter(Pargiter) and Katerina his wife in 1526. There are also several possible versions of the name Haines (viz. Hand, Handes, Handis, Handys, Hanes, Hanne, Hannes, Hannys, Hayne, Haynes, Heyn, Heynes, Heynson, and Heyneys) from 1456 to 1520 mentioned in a large variety of places, the earliest of which seems to be Knowle.

Page	_Year_	
19	1456-7	*Johannes Hannes and Agnetus his wife*
22	1457	*John Heyne and Johanna his wife*
23		*Stephan Hanes and Margeria his wife*
36	1460	*John Harynes and Tibot his wife*
43	1461	*Johannes Handes & Agnus his wife of Stretfort, to pray for their souls*
44	1461	*Robtus Handis & Agnetus his wife*
48	1462	*Johannes Heyne of Loxley & Alicia his wife*
54	1464	*Johannes Hanne & Juliana his wife of Fynyngley*
55	1466	*Agnes Heyne of Balshall widow*
75	1469	*Edmund Handys of Beley & Margareta his wife*
		Johannes Handys & Jon pray for the soul of Jon
107	1493	*Degre heynes Bayly of Warwyke*
127	1498	*Johannes heynson & Alicia his wife of Barkiswelle*
139	1500	*Johannes Hanne & Johanna his wife of Yerdeley*
140	1500	*Johannes Hannes & Elnoria his wife of Collishille*
160	1504	*Johannes Hannys & Emmot his wife for parents William & Johanna*
		Johannes Hannys of Shawell
161		*Johannes Hannys & for the souls of his parents of Ofchirche*
166		*Johannes Hand & Christina for the souls of Thome & Ysabella*
177	1506	*Thomas Haynes of Royton*
219	1514	*John Hynde & Johanna his wife for the souls of Richard and Johanna of chadston & gaydon*

This book also contains many other names with an early connection to Haines's in colonial America, mostly Quakers who married into the Haines line. There are several different spellings of surnames Barnard, Hiatt, Middleton, Pargiter, Parkins, Reynolds, Roberts, Stokes, Wood, Wodhull, Wright and Young.

I also searched *The Records of Henley in Arden,* the other noteworthy old book I discovered which was transcribed and edited by *Frederick C. Wellstood, M.A., from the original manuscripts for William John Fieldhouse, Esq., J.P., C.B.E., Lord of the Manor of Henley in Arden,* to see if John/1's eldest son, Richard may be mentioned somewhere within it's pages. In the Historical Introduction of this book I find

> *The old market town of Henley in Arden in the county of Warwick is situated in pleasant well-wooded country in the hundred of Berlichway, on the main road from Oxford to Birmingham,... It is 102 miles from London, 8 north from Stratford-upon Avon and 14 south from Birmingham.*

Apparently Henley in Arden did not exist at the time of the Domesday survey. The lands which now form the township and manor were then included in those of Wooten Wawen a manor which, before the Conquest, was under the Lordship of Wagene or Waga as he is called in Domesday, and from whom the place derives part of it's name. 'Wooten', a town in the wood, and 'Wawen', a Middle English distinctive addition from the name of its last Saxon possessor, according to the author. The Conquerer stripped all Waga's possessions from him and granted them to Robert de Tonei, otherwise de Stafford, who then made a grant of them to Thurstan de Montfort, a kinsman of Henry of Newburgh, first Earl of Warwick. This was the first of the de Montforts to settle at Donnelie, where he built his castle and called it Beaudesert. From this time on the adjoining manors of Henley and Beaudesert were destined to be frequently held by the same lord. Sometime between 1135 and 1154, Thurston de Montfort obtained from the Empress Maud a charter granting him the right to establish in his castle at Beaudesert a market to be held weekly on Sunday, and it goes on to say that it is doubtless that "from the establishment of this weekly market...the town of Henley in Arden took it's origin."

In this ancient book, which is a chronological history of the manor courts held annually at Henley from 1546 to 1918, I went through every page line by line, most of which were written in Latin. I was looking for any form of the name Haines (viz. Hand, Handes, Handis, Handys, Hanes, Hanne, Hannes, Hannys, Hayne, Haynes, Heyn, Heynes, Heynson, and Heyneys) from the earliest known history after the Conquest, but finding no success until the year 1606. There was not one mention of any form of the name Haines before that. Several family names that later married into the Haines line did show up in the pages, however:

30 Aug 1484 John Stokes, p. x

16 may 1508 Rouland Stokes and William Raynaldys, p. xi

Feb. 1546 Philip Stokes and Joan Stokes, widow. p. xv

1376 William de Beauchamp

1546-7 Thomas Wryght, Thomas Yatte, Anna Yatte and Thomas Stokes

1592 Margareta Knoles

1598 John Wright

1608 Thomas Wood

Finally, on page 62, I did find a Richard Hands. It was within the list of Henley in Arden freeholders names on the "Henley Suit Role 1606", dated 22 October 1606. But there was a footnote on this name saying "lined through". 22 October 1606 was one whole year minus a day before John/1 was buried at Swerford. This could not have been John/1's son, Richard. He was only ten years of age in 1606. But it could have been his father. And it was probably "lined through" because he had died since the previous "Henley Suit Roll" was taken. Unfortunately, I find no earlier list of freeholders in the book. There was a Jone Heaynes, widow, as well, also lined through in this list. Was this Richard's wife or mother? His sister, perhaps?

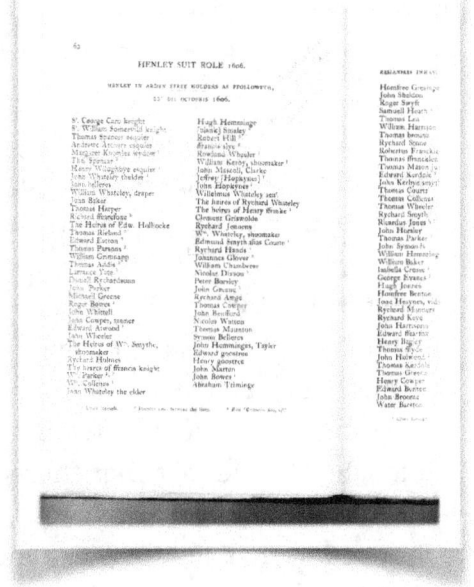

Then, on page 66, the manor court of 21 October 1607, just one year minus a day later, there was a

> presentmente at court made by the cunstables concerning the breach of
> the peace

at Henley in Arden which stated

> Manton[and] William Whatley,xij d., shumaker, for breking the
> peace We present Peter Manton, xij   d., Thomas Manton,
> Elizabeth vppon John Haynes and the same John had a
> bloudshed but who gaue the blodshed we knowe not.

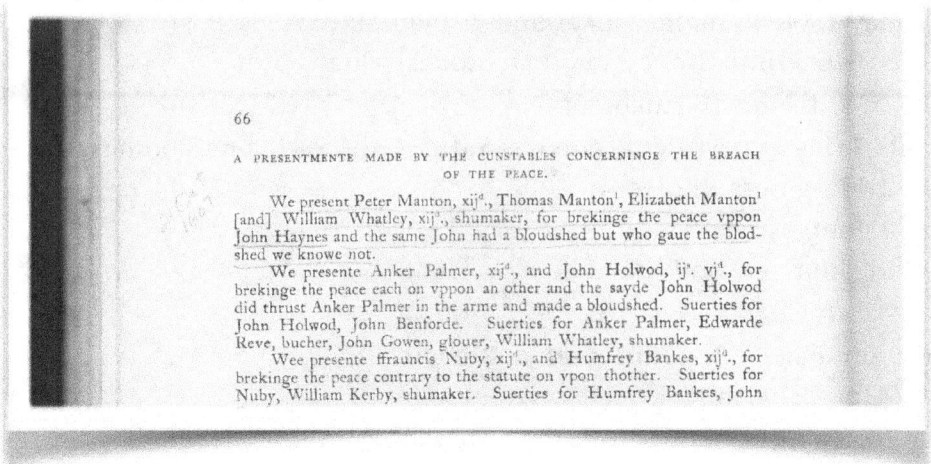

A PRESENTMENTE MADE BY THE CUNSTABLES CONCERNINGE THE BREACH
OF THE PEACE.

We present Peter Manton, xij^d., Thomas Manton¹, Elizabeth Manton¹ [and] William Whatley, xij^d., shumaker, for brekinge the peace vppon John Haynes and the same John had a bloudshed but who gaue the blodshed we knowe not.

We presente Anker Palmer, xij^d., and John Holwod, ij^s. vj^d., for brekinge the peace each on vppon an other and the sayde John Holwod did thrust Anker Palmer in the arme and made a bloudshed. Suerties for John Holwod, John Benforde. Suerties for Anker Palmer, Edwarde Reve, bucher, John Gowen, glouer, William Whatley, shumaker.

Wee presente ffrauncis Nuby, xij^d., and Humfrey Bankes, xij^d., for brekinge the peace contrary to the statute on vpon thother. Suerties for Nuby, William Kerby, shumaker. Suerties for Humfrey Bankes, John

There is no further detail about this 'blodshed' on John Haynes, about when or how exactly it happened; but the 'presentment' at court concerning this 'blodshed' does occur just one month after the 23 Sep 1607 burial of John/1.

Could this 'blodshed' have been the cause of John/1's death in September? Yes, I think so. Perhaps 'blodshed' was a medieval colloquialism for murder back then. But even if it was not murder, but just serious injury, uncontrolled bleeding or a fatal infection might likely have occurred following the 'blodshed.' The fact that there were four people involved, but "who gave the bloodshed we know not" might explain why the matter appeared to have been dropped at that time and the four perpetrators not mentioned again. But I do find Peter Taunton mentioned several times later in the book, and there may be other records that contain the information. I have wondered about the cause of John/1's death since first finding his will. And this must be it. But I still wonder about the perpetrators.

He was still a young man with a young family in 1607. Taking the probable 1589 or 1590 date of his marriage at about age 25, the average age for a young man to marry at that time into account, he was probably only about forty years of age in 1607. Thus an accident is a very probable cause of his death. I say he was probably married in 1589 or 1590 because his first child, daughter Susannah, was born in 1591. So yes, I believe the 'blodshed' at Henley in Arden could very well have been the reason for his early death. He was probably at Henley in Arden to attend the manor court on the property inherited from his father, Richard Hands, who is named, but crossed out, on the rent list of Henley in Arden freeholders in 1606.

Richard Hands had apparently died sometime before the rent list was brought up at the Manor Court in 1606 and, since he was no longer living, crossed out. Since all freeholders were required to attend their Manor Court, Richard Hands' son and heir, John/1, was probably at Henley in Arden for that purpose about the time of the annual "View of Frankpledge with Court Baron", also known as the Manor Court, was to occur in 1607.(See explanation of Manor Courts following)

Manorial Courts
The lord of the manor could hold two courts:

Court Baron
This was obligatory and dealt with transference of copyhold land, enforcing local customs and agricultural practice and settling minor disputes and debts involving less than 40 shillings. The land records of courts baron are discussed in the section on Inheritance of Land, and Sale and Transfer of Land.
Court Leet
There may also have been a court leet (including the view of frankpledge) which was essentially a subsidiary hundred court. It dealt with criminal offences such as murder, treason, rape, arson, counterfeiting and burglary, which it then referred on to the county assizes, as well as common law offences for which it levied punishments, and it also appointed some local officials.

In practice the two courts were usually held on the same day, one after the other, and recorded separately but often in the same manor court roll or book. All tenants of the manor had to attend and were fined (amerced) for not doing so. Although the customs of holding land varied greatly from manor to manor there were uniform standards of procedure and practice of record keeping, which simplifies their use by the researcher. The manorial system became extinct in 1922 on the demise of copyhold land, but many manors had replaced copyhold much earlier and no longer held courts. Other local courts, mention of which may be found amongst manor records, include:

Hundred (division of a county) courts
Pie Powder (market) courts from pieds poudreux = dusty feet.
Portmote (port) courts
Swainmote (forest) courts
Woodmote (woods) courts

The "blodshed" did occur before 21 October 1607 when the presentments were made at court. Therefore, it seems possible, even probable, that this John Haynes was the John Hannes (John/1) who died and was buried 23 September,

1607 in the church at Swerford, just one month before the perpetrators of the 'blodshed' at Henley in Arden were presented at court.

The aforementioned Elizabeth Haynes who wrote her will 17 Oct 1606 may have been the widow of the Richard Hands whose name was lined through in the Freeholders rent list of the Manor of Henley in Arden on 22 October. I do not yet know when Richard Hands died, but it definitely would have been before the 21 October Manor Court in 1606, and Elizabeth claims to be 'sick of body' in her own will written just days before that Manor Court. What was the cause of their demise? Richard died before the 21 October, 1606 Manor Court and Elizabeth died sometime between 17 October, 1606 when she wrote her will, and 19 September, 1607, when the inventory of her property, which I found on Film #173601 at the Family History Library in Salt Lake City, was signed.

I know from the will of Marie Heynes of Kings Sutton, that her deceased husband, Thomas, was definitely Elizabeth's son, but the John Haines who signed Elizabeth's inventory was definitely not Thomas's son. Thomas's wife, Marie(Pargiter), was born 1583 and probably married no earlier than the turn of the century, 1600. Therefore, their son, John, who was not her eldest son, could not have been old enough to sign a legal document in 1607. It could, however, have been John/1 who signed the inventory. He was alive to sign the inventory on 19 September 1607, and his burial was recorded just four days later, on 23 September. Elizabeth's will was proven just one day short of four months later, on 18 Jan 1607. I have yet to find a burial record for Richard or for Elizabeth, but her inventory was dated 19 September, 1607, and signed by Thomas Haines and John Haines. So she did die before John/1! Oh dear, that means she cannot be John/1's stepmother, the 'mother' to whom he left forty shillings in his will.

But wait a minute! He wrote his will on 10 September, 1607, 9 days before the inventory of Elizabeth's property was signed, and he was buried on the 23rd day of September that same year, just four days after signing the inventory. That means the 'blodshed', if it was in fact murder, must have occurred after the 19th of September and before the 23rd. If, however, the 'blodshed' was injury and not murder, it probably occurred before 10 September, as John/1 says in his will on that day that he is "sick of body", leading me to believe that although he may have been injured, his health those last days after Elizabeth died and before he himself was buried might have been good enough to participate in, and sign her inventory. The injury could have been healing and he growing stronger when a sudden hemorrhage, a blood clot, or results of infection and blood poisoning brought about his sudden death. Or, he may have simply been ailing when he wrote his will, but still a victim of 'blodshed'/ murder after signing Elizabeth's inventory. (See timeline following)

Oct 17, 1606 . . . .Elizabeth writes her will.
                     Richard Hands dies sometime before the 21 Oct Manor Court.
Oct 21 . . . . Manor Court meets
Oct 22 . . . . Freeholders rent list - Richard Hands name is lined through.
Nov
Dec
Jan
Feb
Mar 1606/7
Apr 1607
May
Jun
Jul
Aug . . . . 'blodshed'/injury possibly occurs.
Sep 10, 1607 . . . . John/1, sick of body, writes his will.
Sep 19 . . . . John and Thomas Haines sign Elizabeth's inventory.
                     John/1's 'blodshed'/murder possibly occurs
      or   John/1 dies from previous 'blodshed'/injury.
Sep 23 . . . . John/1 buried
Oct 21 . . . . Presentments at court for "blodshed on John Haines"
Nov
Dec
Jan 18, 1607 . . . . .Elizabeth's will proven.
Feb
Mar 1607/8

Elizabeth, who was "of Kings Sutton" did not mention land in her will. But if Richard Hands of Henley was her husband, he would have already bequeathed the tenancy at Henley in Arden to his son, John/1. And John/1, who died at Swerford in September, 1607, bequeathed that property to his eldest son, Richard, who I believe, was the "Hannes Richd s. John" born 1596 at Swerford, and who may also have been the "Hanns Richd. s. John"who died at Barford in 1666.

As I said before, this could be the Richard Haynes and Elizabeth Palmer who were married on 15 Nov 1581 at Swerford, and I give the following possibilities and considerations:

1. Thomas Heynes of Kings Sutton and John/1 who died at Swerford, could both be Richard Hands' sons by a first wife, Susan or Susanna, who died sometime before November 1581 when Richard married Elizabeth; but I have yet to find a Richard and Susan marriage or a Susan or Susanna death.

2. Perhaps the George Hannes that was christened on 27 October 1581 was the son of that possible first wife, Susan, who may have died as a result of his birth. It does not seem likely that Richard would have married Elizabeth so soon after the death of Susan, but it's not impossible. Or, George could have been the child of Richard and Elizabeth, but born 3 weeks or so before their marriage ceremony also not impossible. Actually it was not uncommon in early times.

3. Perhaps Richard and Elizabeth were not George's parents. The parish records say only that on 27 Oct 1581 "Hannes, Geo (was) chrystened". No parents were named.

4. There was also a "Rychard Hannes" christened at Swerford on what appears in the ancient records to be 15 Apr 1587. This could have been the brother John/1 named in his will. Although John/1 did mention a brother, Richard, in his will, Elizabeth did <u>not</u> mention a son, Richard, in hers.

5. Upon becoming widowed, Elizabeth might have moved to Kings Sutton, where she lived when she wrote her will, to be with her son, Thomas, and his wife Marie (Pargiter) Heynes. Marie may have been an heiress to tenancy on the Manor of Kings Sutton, as the Pargiter family was known to be quite well off in and around Northamptonshire. Thomas would have had 'free bench' to Marie's inherited tenancy, and it would have gone to her youngest son on Thomas's death. But wait a minute! Marie was a widow, therefore her youngest son would have already received her inherited property upon her husband, Thomas's, death. She did leave everything else to her son, John, after he paid her bills and executed her estate.

I know that Marie's eldest son was Richard, so was Thomas her youngest son? Or was John her youngest son? She does not say in her will. If John Heynes was her youngest son, and she was heiress to Kings Sutton property, he would have inherited that property when his father died. And if he, Marie's son John, fathered the brothers John and my Richard Haines, it would account for how John Haines who died in 1680 got the property he left to my Richard. I did say at the beginning of this paper that Marie's son John was the right age to be father to my Richard, but I have not yet found evidence of his marriage or records of any children he may have fathered.

It does appear, however, that Marie's son, John, may indeed have been heir to Kings Sutton property, but apparently left no progeny. That would leave the inheritance of Kings Sutton property to the next-in-line family member, which Wikipedia, the internet free encyclopedia, maintains "the son of a deceased elder brother inherits before a living younger brother by right of substitution for the deceased heir." and "brothers succeed by seniority of age" subject to substitution. My research has led me to believe, although I have no proof, that John/1 of Swerford and Marie's husband, Thomas Heynes, were brothers.

I find no Richard Haines at all in the Henley in Arden book after the lined-through Richard Hands in the 1606 list of freeholders, and no John Haines after the 'presentment' until much later. I find a Robert Haines, aletaster, in October 1627, a Robert Heynes, cloathworker and a Robert Heynes, baker, in October 1637, 1641 and 1643. There is a Joh. Haynes on the jury in October 1673, a Joh. Haynes and a Thomas Haynes in 1675, 1677, and 1699; but these men are probably not in my branch. I believe they may descend from John/1's son, Richard Hannes, who was born 1596 at Swerford and who was left property at Henley in Arden by John/1 in 1607. He may be the "Rchd. s. John (who) died at Barford" 28 Jan 1666. In Oxfordshire, there is a Barford St.Michael located 3.47 miles east of Swerford, a Barford St.John located 4.41 miles also east of Swerford, and a Burford, located 14.06 miles southwest of Swerford. In Warwickshire, there is a Barford located 10.60 miles southeast of Knowle.

I have found Haynes wills in Worcestershire which contain family members who match what I know about my people; but I wonder if there is any possibility that my Haines family would have, or even could have migrated to a different county as early as the fifteenth century. If any of these Haynes's are related to me, it is not provable at this time. Whether people moved from one county to the other, the county boundaries changed, or just that the Warwickshire records were located at Worcestershire, I do not know. It is only a few miles distant, and I did find some Haynes wills there. One of particular interest is a Richard Haynes who died in 1555 leaving property to his wife, Jone, and son, Richard. The same names that were 'lined through' in the the 1606 Henley in Arden records. This Richard leaves to his son, Richard, the *"lease that I hold of William Haynes for the years to come."* He does not say where this lease is located. Why not Henley in Arden?

In the name of God amen the last day of January in the year of our lord God 1555 I Richard Haynes of the parish of Grafton Flyford in the county of Worcestershire being perfect in mind and good remembrance make this my last will and testament in manner and form following . First I commit my soul unto almighty god my maker and redeemer

...desiring the merits of Christ's passion and my blessed lady Saint Mary and all the   saints of heaven to pray for me and my body to be buried in the churchyard of Grafton Flyford.

Item I bequeath unto my parish church --(money)

Item I bequeath unto Richard my son my lease that I hold of William Haynes for the years yet to come.   This I give my free land unto Jone my wife during her life and after to remain to Richard my son and to his heirs.   (Except one half acre that I give to William my son and his heirs that profit on --?--) and another half an acre I give unto George my son and his heirs extending upon ----well?---.

Item I bequeath unto Henrye my son 20 nobles in lawful money with an heifer and a bullock and that my wife Jone must pay.

Item I bequeath unto Jone my daughter 20 nobles and an heifer with her mother's good reward and that I will that Richard my son shall pay.

Item I bequeath unto Elizabeth Bayles my daughter my best brass pot after my wife's decease

Also I bequeath unto George my son 20 shillings and to Wm. my son 20 shillings whom I make my overseers of this my testament.

Item I bequeath to Jone my wife her chamber with all household stuff and implements

Also I give to Richard Haynes George Haynes son an heifer --- delivered

Also I give to William my son's two daughters my (measurement of) barley

and to   William Bayles Thomas Bayles son one (measurement of) barley

The rest of my goods unbequeathed my debts and funeral honestly kept I give to Jone my wife and Richard my son the health of my soul and all christian souls and I also ordain and make Jone my wife and Richard my son jointly my executors

Witness
George Haynes
.... clerk
William Haynes

Proven 19 Feb 1555/6
27 pounds 8 shillings 8 pense -- value of estate

Facts from this will are charted here showing the possibility of a connection to Richard of Henley in Arden.

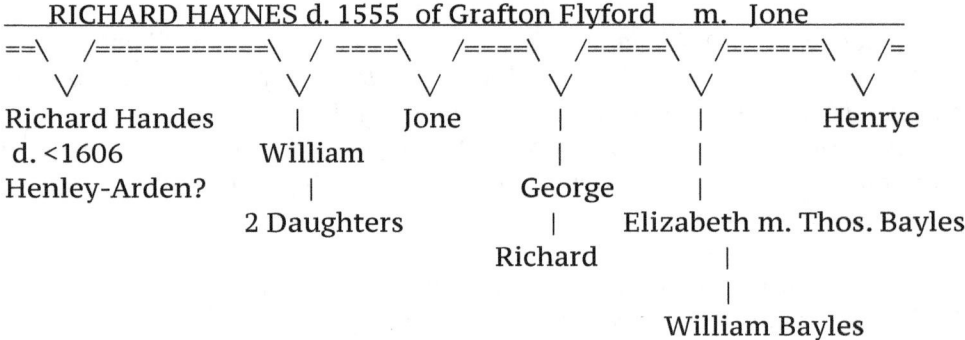

This Richard Haynes was a member of Grafton Flyford Parish in Worcestershire, and he may or may not be my ancestor, but on the chance that he is, I call him Richard/1. In his will he mentioned his wife, Jone and a son, Richard, who I call Richard/2. Richard /2 was to have his father's free land after the decease of his mother, Jone, but the will does not say where that free land was located. It may have been located at Henley in Arden, and Richard/1 could have been the Richard Handes whose name was 'lined-through' in the 1606 Henley manor records. That means Jone, wife of Richard/1, may have been the Jone Handes who was also lined through in that old book.of records. Or it could have been his daughter, Jone, also mentioned in the will. Richard Handes would have been the right age to be the father of John/1 who was buried at Swerford in 1607, and who left property at Henley in Arden to his first son Richard. This first son of John/1 was Richard, born 15 July 1596, and I call him Richard/3. Richard/3 was bequeathed land at Henley in Arden by John/1 in 1607. Possibly, this land at Henley in Arden was the "lease that (he, Richard/1) held of William Haynes for the years yet to come."

I originally began the pedigree outline with Elizabeth of Kings Sutton who died in 1607 because I feel strongly that she may have been John/1's stepmother. And as my writing progressed, I realized I could also connect her to Richard of Henley in Arden as well as Richard of Grafton Flyford. Richard of Henley in Arden, who could have been Elizabeth's husband, was in my mind, almost certainly John/1's father. Although Elizabeth died within days of John/1, she wrote her will the year before, on 17 Oct 1606. That would have been just four days before the scheduled 1606 Manor Court at which all tenants of the manor were required to attend. Perhaps the recent death of her husband, Richard, if Richard Hands of Henley in Arden was her husband, as well as her own claim to be "sick in body but of perfect mind" made it seem necessary for her to write her will at that time.

I believe the reason she did not mention John/1 in her will was because he had already received his share, the property at Henley in Arden from Richard Hands, his father and her husband. As the eldest son, John/1 would have received the bulk of his father's estate, that estate being property in Warwickshire, the estate he bequeathed to his eldest son, Richard/3, in 1607. The fact that John/1 asked in his will to be buried in the church, which was costlier than in the churchyard where most people were interred, also attests to his wealth.

The 1581 marriage of Richard Haynes and Elizabeth Palmer at Swerford opened the possibility of their being the parents of John/1 Hannes who died in 1607. But he had given his second daughter the name Elizabeth, not the first as would be expected if Elizabeth had been his mother. And then, I noticed that this John/1 Hannes had his first child in 1591, therefore he must have been born at least as early as 1570, and probably earlier. That means Richard and Elizabeth would have been married at least eleven years after the probable birth date of John/1 Heynes, and therefore he could not have been their son. John/1 named his first daughter Susanna, and that also, did not fit the expected pattern. But wait a minute! There may be a plausible explanation. Maybe his birth mother was a Susan who had died young, and Elizabeth was his stepmother. Elizabeth's son, Thomas, who had married Mary Pargiter, also named one of his daughters Susan. I believe John/1 and Thomas were brothers. They could both be sons of Richard and his first wife, Susan. Or, since tradition sometimes says that the first daughter in a second marriage is named for the deceased first wife, Thomas could be Elizabeth and Richard's by birth as her other children appear to be. The question is: If Elizabeth was John/1's stepmother, why was she of Kings Sutton when she died? Why not Swerford where John/1 had been buried? She may have gone to live at Kings Sutton with her son, Thomas, and his family when she became the widow of Richard/2 sometime before October, 1606.

The fact that John/1 did bequeath "tenement and lands lying and being in Henley in Arden" to his eldest son, Richard/3, indicates that he, himself, had inherited or been given ownership of that property. Which, according to some forms of England's practice of primogeniture, determines that inherited property must go to the eldest son upon the father's death. This definitely indicates John/1 having family connections in Warwickshire.

Phillipp, John/1's named wife and executrix in his will, was surely not his first wife, or even the mother of his children, except possibly of Edith, born 1605. Phillipp may have been an heiress to a tenancy at Swerford, and John/1's marriage to her would have been the reason they were living there. The name Phillipp does not appear in any of his children or grandchildren or in any of the records until sixty-three years later in 1670 when a Philip Hanns, who might have been a descendant of Phillipp and John/1, married Ric. Huggens of Enston - t.p. Lic.

John/1's youngest son, Edward, whose birth on 1 September, 1602, is listed in the Swerford Parish Register, was named heir to Flaxbutts Field in Knowle,

Warwickshire. And as stated above, the youngest son must inherit his deceased mother's property, suggesting that she came from there, and that John/1 had probably married there the first time. We know from the parish records that the family lived in Swerford, or at least were members of Swerford Parish, from 1591, when John/1's first child was born, until 1607 when he died. And his sons, John/2 and Edward, did remain there to raise families. Sarah, youngest daughter of John/2, was born there in 1641. As were her siblings, John/3 who died in 1680, and my Richard, who emigrated in 1682. They were young children in 1641 and must have been living there also.

The Swerford Parish records list no Haineses before 1581 when Geo. Hannes was born and "Haynes Richd married Palmer, Eliz.", and very few before 1591 when Susan was born. In 1582 an "Eliz., wid.", married and an Anthony Haines was buried. In 1583 a John Heynes was buried. The next page is partly illegible, but had at one time any or all of the years 1585 and 1586 on the left hand page, and probably 1587, where the birth of a Richard Hannes on 15 April 1596 is recorded at the top of the right hand page. The written number of the year 1588, is at the center of the page.(see p. 38) In 1589 an Agnes Hanes married and an Agnes Heynes was buried. In 1590 an Eliz Hanns married. Since there are so many Haines's of so many different spellings in and around that area, it may never be known if any of these people really do fit into John/1's family.

These Swerford records reveal a dearth of John and/or Richard Haines Hand, Handes, Handis, Handys, Hanes, Hanne, Hannes, Hannys, Hayne, Haynes, Heyn, Heynes, Heynson, or Heyneys after the year 1641 when Sarah was born to John/2. John/2 was born 1599, and I believe his wife was the Anne Haynes who was buried 1674 under the care of Banbury Monthly Meeting of the Society of Friends. The year 1641 was probably about when this branch of the family left Swerford in western Oxfordshire for Banbury on the eastern border near Aynhoe and Kings Sutton, both of which were located nearby in Northamptonshire. Their nine-mile migration may have been because of the civil war that was raging at that time, or possibly because my Richard's brother, John, was next in line to inherit land at Kings Sutton as mentioned earlier.

The Swerford records prove that Edward was born in 1602, his sister Eeedith(sic) in 1605, and that their father, John/1, died in 1607. John/1's will proves that Phillipp was his wife in September, 1607. It is possible that:
1. Edward's mother, Edith or Marie died after 1602 leaving John/1 free to marry Phillipp.

2. Eeedith(sic) could be the daughter of Phillipp who John/1 might have married shortly after the birth of Edward in 1602 and the death of his first wife, Edith or Marie.

3. Edward's mother, Edith or Marie, may have died in childbirth. Edward did give his first daughter the name, Edith, which could mean that his mother was Edith, or, as mentioned earlier, he might have named this first daughter for his sister, Eeedith(sic). Unfortunately the parish register does not mention the mother's name in these early cases.

I know that John Haines, born 1625 and died 1680, and who I call John/3, lived and had property in Northamptonshire, as it was stated in his will that he was "of Kings Sutton". And his property,

> *all that part of my messuage in Kings Sutton aforesaid which is free land and not held by copy of court roll and also all my airable land round lying and being in the fields of Kings Sutton aforesaid and in Astrope in the said county of Northampton which...copy of court roll with all and singular the appurtenances to the same belonging*

was located in areas around Kings Sutton, and according to The Banbury Historical Society's *KINGS SUTTON Northamptonshire CHURCHWARDENS' ACCOUNTS 1636-1700,*

> *The parish of Kings Sutton covered both the village of Kings Sutton, which then had a population of about 500-600, and also the hamlets of Astrop and Walton and parts of Purston and Charlton. Other parts of Purston and Charlton were in the parish of Newbottle.*

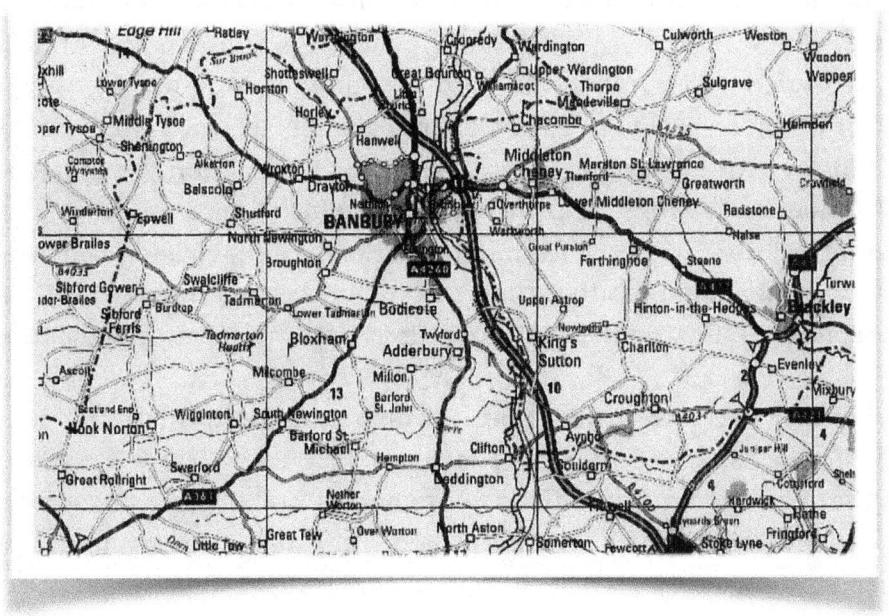

Parish and land records also show that my Richard Haines could be the one baptized in 1635 at Swerford, and that he was 'of Northamptonshire', even while being a registered member of the Banbury Monthly Meeting of Friends. My Richard and his wife, Margaret were living at Charlton and recorded members of Newbottle Parish in 1661 and 1663, living at Aynhoe and recorded members of St Michaels Church in Aynhoe from 1665 to 1672, and recorded members of the Banbury Quaker meeting while still living at Aynhoe from 1673 until 1682 when they emigrated.

These two brothers, John and Richard Hannes, are recorded in Swerford Parish records as grandsons of John/1 who died in 1607. In ten years searching English records, I find them to be the only brothers named John and Richard Haines (Hand, Handes, Handis, Handys, Hanes, Hanne, Hannes, Hannys, Hayne, Haynes, Heyn, Heynes, Heynson, or Heyneys) born at a time and place that would make it likely for them to be my immigrant ancestor and his brother. Since I have yet to find evidence of any marriage and family of John Heynes, son of Thomas and Marie (Pargiter) Heynes of Kings Sutton, I believe that John/1 Hannes who was buried at Swerford in 1607 is the grandfather of my Richard who died at sea in 1682.

I also strongly believe, because people tend to gather and settle with others of their family or chosen community, that my Richard's parents were also members of the Society of Friends there at Banbury. In the minutes of that Monthly Meeting, the death of a John Haynes in 1672 and an Anne Haynes, widow, in 1674 is recorded. I believe these people may have been John and my Richard's parents, John/2 Hannes born 1599 at Swerford, and his wife, Anne. I believe this even though I have yet to find a record of their marriage or a registered birth for Anne. I believe they probably joined the Society of Friends about 1673, around the same time their son, my Richard joined. Again, I believe this parentage because of their naming patterns as well as location. My Richard's previously unknown eldest daughter was born in 1661 at Charlton and given the name Anna. His brother John's 1680 will reveals that he also had a daughter named Anne, that she was named first in the will, and therefore may be the eldest daughter. This leads me to believe that their mother's name may have been Anne or Anna. They both named their eldest sons John, with Richard being their choice for second son's names.

I will call this John, born 1625, John/3. He was an eldest son, but his father was John Hannes, born 1599, the one I call John/2. This John/2 was the second son of John/1, and he did not inherit property. John/1 bequeathed 20# in money only, to John/2 and all his sisters equally after leaving inherited property in Warwickshire to both his eldest and his youngest sons.

That means John/3 and my Richard were not in line to inherit property. Another possible reason for my Richard to emigrate. But John/3's will revealed that he in fact, did own property when he died in 1680, property in and around Kings Sutton, which he instructed his brother and others to sell after his death. I wonder how he acquired

> *all that part of my messuage in Kings Sutton aforesaid which is free land and not held by copy of court roll and also all my airable land round lying and being in the fields of Kings Sutton aforesaid and in Astrope in the county of Northampton*

which he gave to his brother Richard of Banbury in 1680. Perhaps he had purchased it with money he inherited from his father, John/2, who was bequeathed only money and no property from his own father in 1607.

Kings Sutton Churchwardens's Accounts, contain the earliest Kings Sutton church records available at that time, and there was a Thomas Haynes on the 1636 Kings Sutton Levy list. This was probably Marie Heynes's son who was mentioned in her 1633 will. Since it also says "page torn and missing", her other sons could have originally been listed there and since lost. But the name John Haynes does not appear at all in this book until 1642.

Also on that 1636 Levy list were surnames Yeats and Pargiter, Marie's family names; as well as Bricknell and Clements, names mentioned in the will of John/3 Haynes who died in 1680. These names were then on each Kings Sutton Levy every year through 1641 when the name Richard Haines disappears from the records and is not entered again until 1662 when it is listed as a tenant of Mr. Cartwright on the Astrope Levy. The Richard who disappeared in 1641 was possibly Marie's son Richard who may have left Kings Sutton Parish if or when he married Emma of Helmdon, or he may have been a casualty of the civil war which was raging at that time. I believe the Richard who reappears in 1662 must certainly be my Richard, as my Richard was 'of Charlton' in 1661 and 1663 when his first two children were baptized at Newbottle Parish, and Charlton and Newbottle were definitely part of Kings Sutton Parish at that time.

I have found no evidence of Marie's son, John, aside from being executor of her will.   He could be the John Haynes who appears in the *Kings Sutton*

Churchwardens' Accounts in 1642 and remains in the book regularly until at least the late 1670's, but if this is Marie's son and not John/2 who was born 1599 or John/3 who died in 1680, he should have been on the 1636 levy list. He was old enough to execute her will in 1634, and If he was a tenant of Kings Sutton or other nearby manor he would certainly have been on the levy list as a member of Kings Sutton Parish. Since a John Haynes does not appear in the Kings Sutton churchwarden's book until 1642, I believe it could very well have been John/2, born 1599, who would probably have found it convenient to leave Swerford in Oxfordshire after his youngest daughter, Sarah, was baptized in June, 1641.

There is a John Haynes, Merchant, who died at Banbury in 1643 leaving a wife, Margaret, but no children. I had an idea this John Haynes may have been Marie's son John, but he mentions a Henry Haynes, son of his "late deceased brother Thomas" in his will. Mary did mention a son, Thomas, in her will in 1633, but not a grandson, Henry. It is, however, ten years later, and Thomas could have married and had a son, Henry, after Marie's death. This, John, also mentions daughters of his "late deceased brother William", but here again, there are no 'daughters of' or 'a son, William,' mentioned in Marie's will.

There is a Margaret Haynes, widow, who died of the plague with her maid at Banbury a year later. This Margaret was probably the widow of the aforementioned John Haynes, who mentioned his "beloved wife, Margaret," in his will. She mentions her brother, Robert Turton, but no children to validate a possible connection to Marie's son, John.

I have found no information about what happened to Marie's son, Richard, when he disappeared from the Kings Sutton Levy list. Did he die? Did he move away? Yes, I think he may have moved away to Helmdon, where he may be the Richard Haines who married Emma and whose will was written in 1656 at Helmdon, and is included previously.

The Richard who appears in the Churchwarden's book listed on the Astrope Levy in 1662 could possibly be the son of John/3 Haynes who died in 1680, but he, son of John/3, would have been at most, only about 17 years of age in 1662. At first I thought that seventeen years was probably too young to be mentioned on a levy list, but in 2014, I found another little book at Oxfordshire which belies the thought that minors were not expected to pay taxes. On page 32 of *OXFORDSHIRE A Look at the Past,* author, Hilary L. Turner, says "...the poll tax demanded a contribution of fourpence from every person over fourteen." In spite of that information, I still believe it is my Richard, presumably born 1635 at Swerford, who would have been twenty seven years old in 1662. And according to the Newbottle Parish Records, my Richard was 'of Charlton', in 1661 and 1663, when his two oldest children were baptized there. Charlton is located very near Astrope and Kings Sutton, being "partly in Kings Sutton Parish."

On my previously mentioned July, 2013 trip to England, I also visited the Northampton Public Record Office and found transcriptions of *Kings Sutton Marriages 1570-1837,* in which is listed an Anna Heynes married 1577, an Alice Heynes married 1582, a Richard Heynes married 1589, an Elizabeth Heynes married 1598, and a Thomas Heynes married 1601, as well as a John Haynes married 1643. The aforementioned Alice who married in 1582 and Anna who married in 1577 could be Elizabeth's daughter, Alce, and her granddaughter Anne, both mentioned in her 1606 will. The John Haynes who married in 1643 was possibly the John Haynes of Banbury who died in 1643 leaving a widow, Margaret, who died in 1644 of the plague.

At first I thought the 1601 marriage of Thomas Heynes mentioned in these Kings Sutton records might be the marriage of Marie Pargiter, and Thomas Heynes. Marie, who was baptized in 1583 at Aynho, would have been about eighteen years old in 1601. An appropriate age to marry, I thought. But on another page the marriage was listed with the bride's name and it was not Mary Pargiter. Since I had seen her birth recorded there, I searched those Aynho records again. Every line on every page. Her marriage should be recorded there in the parish where she was baptized, but it was not to be found. I think now, that this marriage record may never be discovered, as this copy of the actual records seemed to have several pages missing, and on a few of the pages that were there, some very faded entries which were impossible to decipher.

The John Heynes who married in 1643 could be Marie's son, John, who was the executor of her will. Or it could be John/2, born 1599, or even possibly but unlikely, John/3, who was born in 1625 and died in 1680.

The *Newbottle Parish Records 1538-1812* list under the title HAYNES/HEYNES an Agnes (W) (EDWARDES) married 1540, a Peter, christened 1553; and a Richard, christened 1558; but here again, no parents are named.

The transcript of the *Aynho Births, Deaths, and Marriages 1653-1759* list under the name HAINES/HAINS/HAYNES/HAYNSE/HEANS, none earlier than 1665 or later than 1672 that could be mine. The actual names and dates are:

Margaret (& Richard) cp1665

I do not know what the 'cp' means. The next line has no name but a date, "1666", in the date column followed by a line with the names:
"Margaret (&Richard)" with nothing after. I assume that this Margaret and Richard are meant to be connected to the date 1666 as that is the year their son, Thomas, was baptized. The next line has

"Mary (&Richard) cp1672"

which does not fit my family's profile. I do not have a Richard married to a Mary. Perhaps it is a mistake, or a short form of the name Margaret. It does mention Thomas's 1666 christening further down in the list as well as William's in 1672, both of which are sons of my ancestor, immigrant Richard Haines.

"Margaret (& Richard) c1666", and then a little further down I find:
"William   c 1672."

These transcriptions are confusing. The names and dates are there, but they make no sense. Then I remembered! I had attained photocopies of the Aynhoe Parish records several

years earlier, and went to my sources file to find the parish register copy of Richard's birth.   It was   registered on 6 August 1665, and can barely be made out on the second line from the top of the register copy on the right, and Thomas's birth 22 Dec 1666, on the second line from the bottom of the same copy..   William's 24

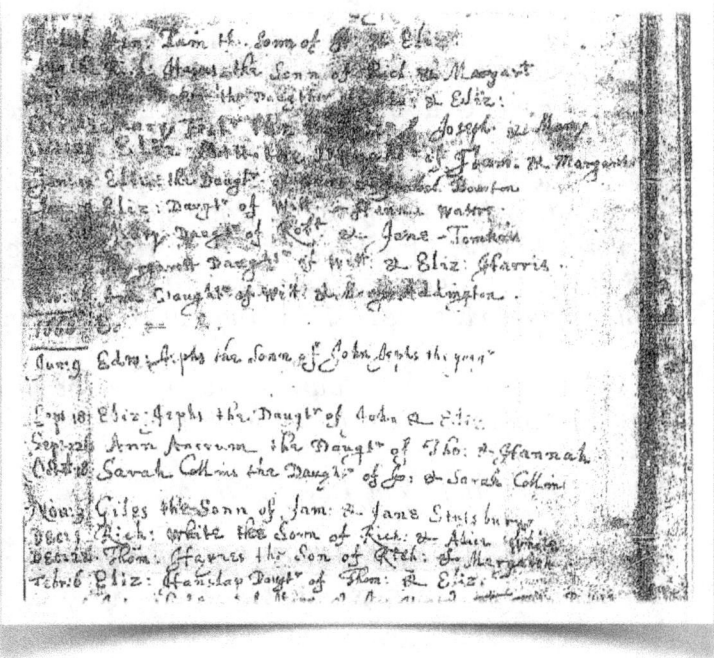

April 1672 baptism is on the third line from the bottom of the lower partial page copy of the Aynhoe parish records shown here. I think the transcriptionists of the original records found it difficult to translate the

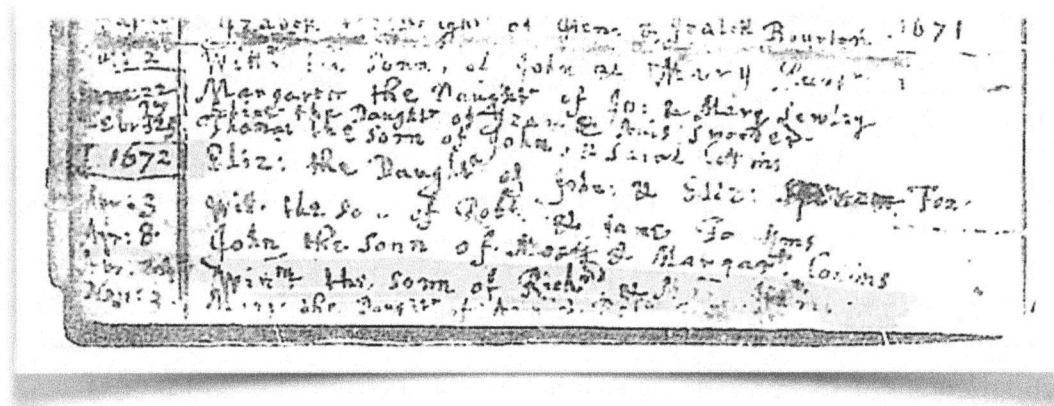

ancient faded writing and came up with incorrect information; but I knew what I was looking for, and "Rich son of Rich and Margaret" and "Willm the son of Rich and Margaret " jumped right out for me. It was fairly clear and unmistakeable on the microfilm.

I found more old Haynes wills in Worcestershire records on microfilm #0932932 at the Salt Lake City library. A John Heynes of Dornston and 'first name illegible ' Haines of Inkbarrow, which may or may not be related to me, but I include them here for future reference.

1548/9 Will of John Heynes of Dornston, Warwickshire

In the name of God Amen on the eleventh day of February (1548/9) in the second year of the reign of our sovereign lord King Edward the sixth by the grace of God king of England France and Ireland defender of the faith and in the church of England and Ireland supreme head I John Heynes of the parish of Dornston in the diocese of Worster make my testament and last will in manner and form following. first I bequeath my soul to Almighty God and my body to be buried in the churchyard of Inkbarrow.

Item I bequeath to William my sonn my land in Bybery in the parish of Grafton after the decease of my brother George Heynes

Item I bequeath to John Heynes William's sonn -----

Item I bequeath to Richard my sonn 2 heifers one red tagged and the other brindle and 40 shillings that his brother George shall give him out of his bequest

Item   I bequeath to Thomas my son a bullock

Item   I bequeath to Anthony Humphrey Heynes (h)is sonn one cow calf

Item   I bequeath to John my sonn 12 pence

Item I bequeath to Robert my son a cow calf of color brown

Item I Bequeath to George Winfield my wife's sonn all the wool of my sheep growing this year

Item I bequeath to Wa(l)ter Balte 6 shillings 8 pence

Item I bequeath to every one of my godchildren a grote apiece

Item I bequeath to William my sonn my violet cote

Item I bequeath to Thomas Heynes my sonn my russet cote

Item I bequeath to Richard Russell my quarter cote and my old doublet

Item I bequeath to Humphrey my sonn my best buckskin doublet

Item I bequeath to Johan   ---   2 stryke of wheat

Item I bequeath to George my brother 1 quarter of malte

All the rest of my goods and   debts   unbequeathed I give and bequeath to Elizabeth my wife and George my sonn whom I ordain and make executors to execute and to fulfill this my testament and last will

Also I make my supervisors of this my last will Henry Eme and Henry Balte

Item to Henry Eme and Henry Balte to whom I bequeath for their pains 5 shillings

Witnesses to this my last will   John Woodward and Harry Eme and Henry Balte and Anthony Balte with others mor.

Probated   value #34

See chart on page 74.

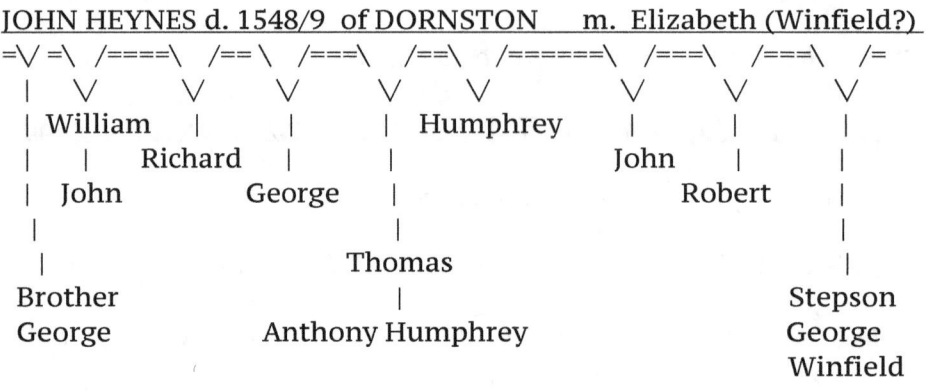

JOHN HEYNES d. 1548/9 of DORNSTON   m. Elizabeth (Winfield?)

Will of ?Haines Inkbarrow, Worcestershire   ?

.....of our lord God

Ly... IN THE COUNTY OF WORCESTERSHIRE

being sick of body but of perfect memory I do ordain and make this my last....

...churchyard of Inkbarrow....

.....west... pence....

Item I bequeath to .... of inkbarrow

Item i bequeath to Alice my daughter and

....Dorothy........

and to be paid at the day of her marriage.....

......George....

......pains......

to be paid at the day of her marriage......

and to be paid at the day of.....

.....to my daughters I will......

.....pot of brass that I had of my mother....

......and I will that Dorothy her sister shall have it....

Bequeath to Eleanor my wife and to Robert my son....executors....

.....two silver spoons

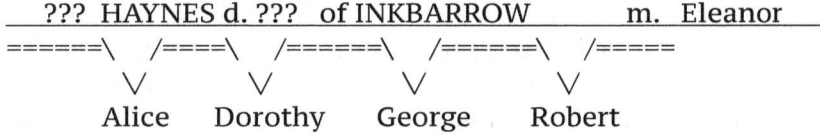

I cannot help but feel that one or more of these Haynes families whose wills I have found in Worcestershire may be connected in some way to my Richard Haines who emigrated in 1682. But why are they living in Worcestershire instead of Oxfordshire, Warwickshire, or Northamptonshire where I am pretty sure they were. These migrations of the John and Richard Haines families recorded here are a point of confusion and mystery to me. I had always, or at least since I learned about the English system of Manors and Manor Courts and how families were tenants on Manors rather than owning or renting private homes as we do here in America, thought that a family lived on the manor for generations with no reason to move to another manor in another area. I have found this system written in other books, that in the beginning and for hundreds of years the land supported all of the people with agriculture and farming, and that families lived for generations as tenant farmers on the same manor. So why was my family, if this is my family, found in so many different places? But then I ran across another little book which may explain it.

In *A SHORT HISTORY OF WARWICKSHIRE AND BIRMINGHAM,* by Vivian Bird, I found Sir Arthur Conan Doyle's fictional onset of the Black Death which had been said by some to be the cause of depopulation and lost villages in England. He wrote:

In the month of July in the year 1348, between the feasts of St. Benedict and St. Swithen, a strange thing came upon England, far out of the east there drifted a monstrous cloud, purple and piled, heavy with evil, climbing slowly up the hushed heaven. In the shadow of that strange cloud the leaves drooped in the trees, the birds ceased their calling, and the cattle and the sheep gathered cowering under the hedges. A gloom fell upon all the land, and men stood with their eyes upon the strange cloud and a heaviness upon their hearts...Then the rain began to fall. All day it rained and all the night and all the week and all the month, until folk had forgotten the blue heavens and the gleam of the sunshine.

It was raining at Lammas-tide and raining at the Feast of the Assumption and still raining at Michaelmas. The crops and the hay sodden and black, had rotted in the fields, for they were not worth the garnering. The sheep had died, and the calves also, so there was little to kill when Martinmas came and it was time to salt the meat for winter. They feared a famine, but it was worse than a famine which was in store for them.

For the rain had ceased at last, and a sickly autumn sun shone upon a land which was soaked and sodden with water. Wet and rotten leaves reeked and festered under the foul haze which rose from the woods. The fields were spotted with monstrous fungi of a size and color never matched before - scarlet and mauve and liver and black. It was as though the sick earth had burst into foul pustules; mildew and lichen mottled the walls, and with that filthy crop Death sprang also from the water-soaked earth. Men died, and women and children, the baron of the castle, the franklin on the farm, the monk in the abby, and the villein in his wattle-and-daub cottage. p.51

Bird said the dramatic impact of this meticulously researched description of the onset of the Black Death is unsurpassed in any fictional writing. But it was not just fictional writing. It actually happened in all of England. The Black Death came in 1348 and returned in 1360, and by 1374 the population in England had dropped by 2,250,000. Yet, he says few of the villages were depopulated by the Black Death. Only six villages were lost before 1400 when that plague had occurred. But by 1485 ninety more were lost, and eighty-four more disappeared later. He says "Depopulation can be traced by the disappearance of a village from the Tax List which, by 1280, was fairly comprehensive" but the Poll Tax population of 1377 remained substantial. After the plague, many previously landless villagers took over vacant holdings. It was their opportunity for advancement, he said, and those paid money wages demanded more or moved away in search of better income. p.55

He also said the Black Death destroyed people, not villages. It was instrumental in bringing an end to the manorial system of serfdom, making human labor a commodity in short supply. Wages rose and conditions changed. Agriculture, which had supported the people of England for centuries, was displaced by sheep farming.

This gave rise to the confused belief that the Black Death killed off entire villages. The disappearance of villages over the next century was not brought about by the Black Death, but rather by landlords clearing their estates of people and their dwellings to make way for more sheep pasture.

Finally! A possible answer to my question of why Haines families which fit the facts I knew about my family seemed to be scattered over England, and why I was unable to find them in one parish for more than one or two generations. I have found wills and parish records of Haines Hand, Handes, Handis, Handys, Hanes, Hanne, Hannes, Hannys, Hayne, Haynes, Heyn, Heynes, Heynson, or Heyneys who fit many of the known patterns of my family living in Worcestershire in 1548 and 1555, Warwickshire in 1606, Oxfordshire from 1591 to 1641, and finally Newbottle, Charlton, Kings Sutton and Aynhoe in Northamptonshire from 1642 until 1682 when my Richard and Margaret emigrated. I know they can't all be related to me, at least not in these later generations. But I do find names, dates, and family situations which fit well with what I do know about my ancestors except for the place where they live. This does finally make some sense to me. I now have a plausible explanation for why my family can be found in so many different places--if this is my family, that is.

In September, 2014, I again had opportunity to visit the archives in England hoping to find provable identity evidence of Richard Haines' parents. At the Northampton archives where I had written ahead to let them know what I was looking for, I found that the attendant there had some original 1600 manor court rolls out on the desk for me to study. I was surprised. These ancient records were actual 17th century documents which had been physically rolled into a tube, hence, the name "court rolls". The tubes/rolls had gotten somewhat crushed during the last 400 or so years, and I was very uncomfortable trying to straighten them out to see what they contained. The attendants didn't seem to be concerned, unlike the attendants at the Oxford office. The documents were written in Latin, but I could see and recognize the typical format of the data I had seen translated and printed in books--the members of the jury were named and presentments were listed. But since these documents were written in Latin as most early ones were, I gave up, thinking I would never be able to make sense of them, and because I was nervous about handling these very old manuscripts. The attendants were very nice and very helpful. They had printed out for me twenty-five or so pages which list the individual Aynhoe Manor Court Rolls they have, each with a snippet of the content contained in each one. Upon going through this list when I got home, I realized that I must go back and try again to read those crumpled court rolls.

I did see one more old (1540) parchment roll at Oxford that first trip, and was brave enough to unroll and photograph it. It was "The Survey of the Parke of Swerford," and I think it was a levy list. Several pages were stitched together with some kind of cord using what appeared to be a neat blanket stitch to form a long document which was then

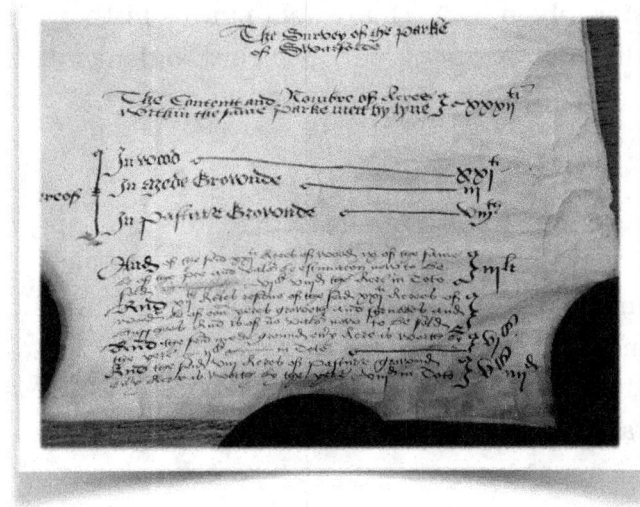

rolled into a tube shape. Is a "Parke" another name for a manor? I wonder. This roll did contain a Thomas Haynes. But it was fifty years before John Hannes' first child was born there in 1591. Could this Thomas Haynes have been any relation to my ancestors? Maybe.

After seeing and photographing this Swerford document, I realized that I could have made out the names and perhaps some details on the Northampton rolls, and wished I had tried harder with those Aynho and Kings Sutton Court Rolls. They may contain information about my Haineses. Richard and Margaret did live there from 1665 until they emigrated in 1682. But then I thought, "I already have copies of the original birth records of their children from the Aynhoe, Newbottle, and Banbury church records." And I had searched diligently but been unable to find anything about their marriage in any of those parish records. Maybe, if I tried again, I could find something about Marie's son, John Heynes of Kings Sutton, in those court rolls. Why was he so hard to trace?

I found another little booklet at the Oxford Archives, the *OXFORD CHURCH COURTS Depositions 1592-1596,* written by Jack Howard-Drake. On page 16, Testamentary number 36 on 11 June 1593 is about debt. It mentions among others, "Richard Hannes of Oxford, resident about 30 years, born at Swerford, aged about 33." That would put his birth at about 1560, fifteen years before the first surviving parish record, but nearer the time I estimate John/1 was probably born. He could be the brother, Richard, that John/1 mentions in his will.

After our visit to the Oxford archives, we stayed in Banbury. A lovely old city where we walked down the tree-lined street to 'Banbury Cross' and found this marvelous statue of a "fine lady on a white horse" with "rings on her fingers and bells on her toes" who welcomed us to town. One local tradition claims that the name of the lord of one of the local Manors was Fiennes, and that the famous nursery rhyme about the 'fine' lady was actually about the lady of Fiennes Manor.

We had lunch at The Reindeer Inn, an ancient historic Pub dating from the early 16th century. The Globe Room of the inn was built in 1637 of old wooden paneling. The names of the Knight family, late 16th century owners, is carved in the gates with the date 1570. We sampled some real old-style Banbury Cakes made from the original medieval recipe. Banbury cakes are a local specialty and have been made in the town since at least the 1500s.

Banbury is the location of the early Quaker Meeting where my Richard first expressed his dissent with the Church of England and joined the Society of Friends sometime between 1672 and 1676, back when the Friends met in the homes of their members. It wasn't until about 1750 that the Banbury Quaker Meeting House was built, and on my previous trip to Banbury, I had only seen it through the locked metalwork gate in the arched doorway of the brickwork fence which surrounded the courtyard .

I wanted to speak with some Quakers and see the inside of the meeting house. So I was at that gate at 10:00 AM on Sunday morning, intending to experience a Quaker silent worship service if possible. A very nice lady whose name I regretfully cannot remember, greeted me warmly and invited me in. A concrete walk curved its way to the entry in which the nice lady greeted members and visitors, and which opened into the hallway of the meeting house, where I did meet and spoke with some local Quakers. At the end of the hallway was the meeting room with chairs arranged in a circle for Sunday meeting of their reduced membership. In one corner of the meeting room stood a beautiful old original hand-crafted Quaker clock.

These Banbury Quakers were so nice and so friendly. They told me about the oldest, built in 1675, Adderbury Meeting House which was located about three miles away on the edge of the Cotswolds, and invited me to attend the afternoon meeting there with them, which I did.

The Adderbury meeting house, as it stands today, is pictured on the next page along with pictures of the inside of the building. First is a photo of an early painting of the original main floor showing the entry and stairway to the gallery. It looks the same today. Next lower is the gallery today, also pretty much unchanged from 1675 when it was new. Look closely at the center right of the lower gallery photo and see the year '1675' carved into the crossbeam.

About twelve or fifteen people were seated on benches when I entered after photographing the outside of the building. They moved aside to make room for me on one bench, and after a few words, the silence took over. It was very peaceful, not unpleasant at all. An hour of total silence, a restful hour for me to contemplate the wonder of sitting in this place where my Richard and Margaret Haines may have sat in silent worship with their family before they emigrated in 1682. No one spoke, although anyone could have. The Quakers believe there is something of God in everyone, and if any member feels the receipt of a message from this essence of God, he or she may break the silence and impart the message for the benefit of all.

These Quakers in this part of England hold a very special meaning for me. I am a member of the eleventh generation of descendants of Richard and Margaret Haines. Until my grandfather, Alvin Haines, married Margaret Kathern Launer, daughter of an Illinois Evangelical Circuit Rider in Portland, Oregon in 1888, my Haines line held over two hundred years of unbroken Quaker heritage. Traditionally, Quakers married only other Quakers, and to do otherwise was cause to be disowned from membership.

Leaving Iowa, where Alvin's father,

Joseph Haines and his mother, Ruth Esther Lupton Haines, had met and married under the care of one of the new monthly meetings they had been instrumental in getting started there in Iowa, and settling in the new and somewhat wild Oregon country, seemed to allow those strict Quaker rules to lose influence over the younger generation. Not only did Alvin marry 'out of unity', but so did two of his brothers, Edward and Oliver. Alvin's sister, Anna Mary, and his younger brother, James, remained unmarried, and moved with their mother to Anna's homestead on Mt. Anne in Aeneas Valley, Okanogan County, Washington where Alvin had also taken out a homestead in 1900.

My research began with the early immigrant Quakers in New Jersey, and after years of reading about all those generations of my family and the Society of Friends, about their traditions and good works, and their silent meetings of worship. I have strong feelings about meeting with these present-day Quakers in England, possible descendants of the original Banbury Quakers in Oxfordshire, where my Richard first joined the Society of Friends. I have not yet been able to actually prove Richard's birth, but I found evidence that seems pretty convincing. And I did find irrefutable evidence of the birth of his eldest son, John, as well as a previously unknown daughter, Anna.

Relics of Medieval Times 9

I was able to go back to England again in 2015, to the Warwick archives first, where I hoped, but failed, to uncover information about the civil war and how it may have effected the every-day life of my ancestors. I wanted to know about John Heynes' family in particular, but was interested in its effect on other tenant families who lived on various Warwickshire manors as well. And second, to the Northampton Archives after writing ahead to let them know which documents I wanted to see, and just like the year before, the documents were there waiting for me. This time I was able to examine the two leather-covered books of original Kings Sutton Parish Records. The covers had gold leaf lettering with the dates 1614 - 1639 on one and 1640 - 1689 in the other. Going through the pages name by name from 1614 to 1660 revealed only one name of interest. It was Johannes Haynes marriage to Elizabeth Sworder on 14 February 1642. This could have been Marie's son, John, but I found no Haines Hand, Handes, Handis, Handys, Hanes, Hanne, Hannes, Hannys, Hayne, Haynes, Heyn, Heynes, Heynson, or Heyneys children's baptisms on later pages. Seems there should have been more Haines' in those Kings Sutton records than I actually found. Perhaps my Haines ancestors had not lived at Kings Sutton for generations as I had once believed, but actually did come from some other location as my research had been hinting all along.

Banbury was the next stop on this trip, and we had reservations at a bed and breakfast a short walk from town. Intending to see the Rollright Stones and the Swerford Church if possible, we took a bus from Banbury to Chipping Norton, another small town near Swerford, and were fortunate to find a very helpful young woman working in a local pub. She contacted a local taxi driver in town who agreed to take us to the Swerford Church and to the Rollright Stones for a flat fee of twenty pounds. I don't remember who it was that told me the Swerford church was still standing, but it was a very exciting moment for me. I was so totally surprised that the church was still there in the first place, and had never in my wildest dreams thought for a moment that I would ever actually walk into the church where my John/1 had been buried almost four hundred and ten years earlier.

Except for the bell tower and steeple, which stood straight like a rocket ready for launch toward Heaven, the church seemed small and distant when first sighted from the bend in the road. It was almost hidden in a grove of large evergreen trees and flanked by several ancient upright gravestones. We walked past a wide, foliage-enclosed, crooked gate that was slightly ajar, and found a path through the gravestones and trees that led to an enclosed dark and cave-like little porch, a covered entranceway of stone that had narrow slate benches on each inner wall. One bench held two small flower pots containing dead remnants of once bright fresh blooms. On the far wall of this dark eery little room our flashlight revealed a gothic-looking, light colored stone doorframe enclosing a large wooden door that was double-hinged and reinforced with two long ironwork braces. The sides of the door and its frame curved gracefully up to a slight peak at the top, and together filled the entire back wall of this musty, dark little vestibule. We approached warily and found the large wooden door unlocked. It swung smoothly open at my touch with an eery silence that seemed unnatural, and we ventured cautiously inside.

The gloomy atmosphere of the entryway seemed to evaporate, and I was immediately struck with a feeling of wonder, almost delight. This little ancient church still had an active congregation. Two rows of dark wooden pews bordered the center aisle. There seemed to be candles everywhere, on every flat surface as well as high up on the walls. Some were nestled in greenery on the sills of each tall beautiful leaded glass window, windows which I had failed to notice from the outside. It was-December 19, and there was a small sparsely decorated Christmas tree near the chancel, evoking a memory of the last, and quite recent, Sunday service along with an anticipatory feeling of Christmas to come. I thought at first, that the inside was very much like every other little old church building I remembered, but when, on returning home and viewing my travel photos, the difference became obvious.. Except for the pews bordering the center aisle, it was definitely not like every old church building in my memory. The exterior

gothic design I had noticed on our approach was repeated on the inside. The narrow door and window openings matched the outside door's pointed arch in design, but they seemed taller, out of proportion to the small floor space. As with the outside steeple, these inside architectural aspects also seemed to be reaching toward heaven. In spite of the darkness, some grave markers in the floor were noticeable (see photos) but none as early as 1607 were visible with our flashlight. Perhaps another visit with a better light and more time might reveal the location of John/1's burial place in the church. The taxi driver said that the outside of the church is almost unchanged since the twelfth century, but the inside had been remodeled sometime during the Victorian era. I wonder when the clock on that outside wall was added.

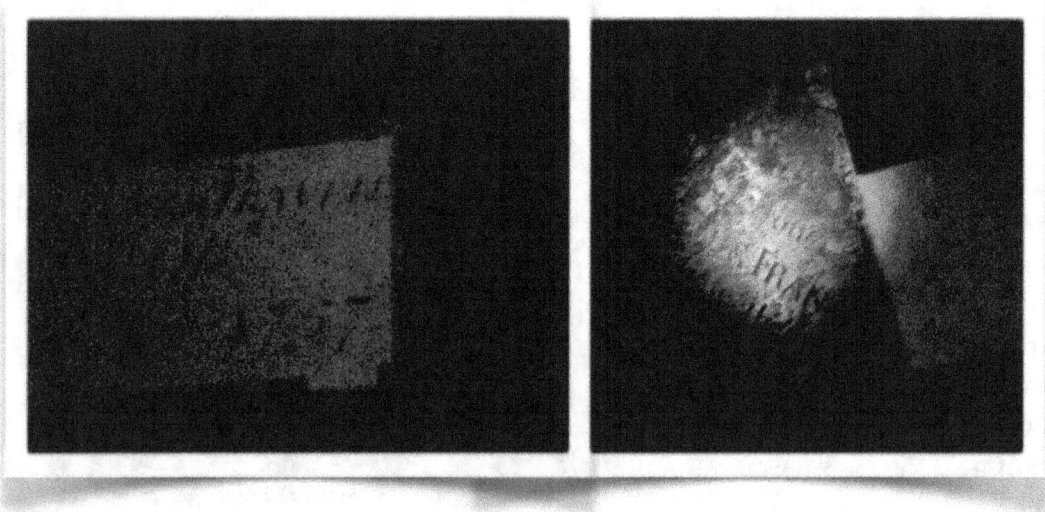

Our next stop on this important little side trip from Banbury was to see the Rollright Stones, a prehistoric megalithic structure similar to Stonehenge located right there on the road from Chipping Norton. The Rollright Stones are said to be older than Stonehenge, and I must say, they did appear so. They were very uneven and weathered, a fair-sized straggling circle of jaggedly eroded rocks. Some almost worn to nothing in the grass while others were up to a few feet tall. Local tradition says that walking the circle and counting the stones more than once, never reveals the same count, and my daughter did

walk the circle and count the stones three times. She counted 70 stones the first time, then 73 and 71 the second and third times.

The King Stone was some distance away across the road, and since it was a wet and rainy day, we decided against walking out into the muddy field for a closer look and snapped pictures from the road. But I did get a closeup of the explanatory sign.

I had read about Rollright Manor and the Rollright Stones many times in my research. I had even found an old Haines will in which the writer claimed to have lived on Rollright Manor, Unfortunately, I could not fit the writer of that will into my known family

Venerable Silent Quaker Meetings   10

I had made plans before leaving home to attend the December 20, 2016 Quaker silent meeting there in Banbury where I had been the year before, and just like the previous year at Adderbury, the hour of silence was peaceful and relaxing, not at all uncomfortable.   And it did, somehow, seem to invoke a mystical essence of God in the room.   One woman spoke for a moment about the universal need for worldwide conservation and environmental protection, and true to their well known title "Friends", at the end of the hour of silence everyone turned in their seats and greeted other attendees seated nearby with a friendly handshake.   Coffee and conversation, during which I learned of the historic significance of the table which centered the room, ended the meeting.   The table, pictured here, had been lost for many decades, but found in some ignominious local place and thankfully, returned to its proper location in this meeting house.   It was known to have been used by George Fox during some of his earliest preachings back in the 1600's when early ancestors of myself and these Banbury Quakers first publicized their dissent with the Church of England and decided to follow his teaching.

Along with my genealogical research, another important reason for this trip to England was to experience the Christmas meeting at the ancient Adderbury Meeting House, which we did that afternoon, on 21 December. My photograph on the next page of a picture which was hanging on the wall inside the meeting house, shows the original arrangement of buildings in which the Adderbury friends met for Sunday worship as well as their monthly business endeavors. The small structure on the left was the women's meeting house which no longer exists, and the building on the right is the the original men's meeting house. The artist's rendition of the property, also pictured on the next page,

shows the original men's building to be identical in physical structure as it stands today.

Women worshipped separately in the early years of the Society. I have seen other early Quaker meeting houses having the women's side and the men's side of the main room. This being one of, if not the earliest, of Friends meetings, a whole separate building for the women was apparently required. The larger building in the photo was the men's place of worship.

This sturdy little meeting house has withstood the test of time. It was built in 1675, by wealthy non-conformist, Bray Doyley, Lord of the Manor at West Adderbury for the local chapter of the Society of Friends. That being the Adderbury Monthly Meeting, which was established in 1656. It is currently equipped with benches on both sides and the back of the room, all facing the center of the first floor area. There is a narrow staircase leading to the gallery above with more benches placed around an opening in the floor of that second level gallery which is fenced all around for safety, but open so that any spoken words from either floor can be heard throughout. Mr. Doyley built the meeting house on his own land at his own expense, and then spent two months in prison for doing so.

Except for being slightly altered by the addition of a cast iron stove inserted in the stone fireplace opening to make it habitable for refugees during World War II, but left cold and unused today, the building is virtually unchanged in over three hundred years. It has no heating system, electric lights, or plumbing conveniences.

For this special Christmas meeting, some members brought blankets to pad the benches, candles for light, and portable gas heating stoves for the comfort of attendees. Near

the end of the hour of Quaker silence, during which one elderly member spoke from scripture, families with children arrived with more candles and holiday creations made by those children.   We were served tea from thermos containers and English christmas cakes before settling down to singing old fashioned Christmas carols accompanied by a lovely string quartette. It was an authentic Quaker Christmas celebration, full of music, good cheer, and friendliness following the traditional silent worship. The perfect way to end a stay in England. I flew home the next day.

Plausible Conclusion 11

After writing and re-writing, reading and re-reading my own words this last year along with re-studying and re-analyzing copies and transcripts of old wills and parish records hoping to prove a Swerford Kings Sutton connection, I finally am ready to end it. While doing all these re-readings and re-writings a small germ of inspiration was growing in the back of my mind. And then I had the most exciting 'ah ha' moment yet.

Right from the day I found Marie Heynes' 1633 will I knew that her son, John, was a very good candidate to be father of my Richard. He had brothers Richard and Thomas, names my Richard had given two of his own sons. And he lived at an appropriate time within a few miles of the last place I knew my Richard to be, Aynhoe and Banbury in the counties of Northamtonshire and Oxfordshire, where his children were born.

But, in spite of spending years searching every film, fiche, and book in libraries and archives in England and in America, which hinted at revealing any small detail about him or his family, my efforts went totally unrewarded. John Heynes of Kings Sutton, who was named executor in his mother, Marie Heynes' will in 1634, seemed to disappear from the earth. I just couldn't find any provable marriage or death record for him. If I could have found proof of his death, it would have allowed what I wanted to be true. I wanted those perfect Swerford parish records to hold the answer to a mystery that every descendant of my Richard who is interested in the family genealogy wants to know. Whether or not John/1 Heynes who was buried in the church at Swerford on 23 October 1607 was absolutely and finally, my Richard's grandfather.

Then, upon seeing the 1680 will of John Haynes, who I knew was definitely brother to my Richard and definitely of Kings Sutton where Marie had lived and died, I became very confused. The timing was just barely possible for this John Haynes to be Marie's son. Marie's son would have been well into his eighties and his brother, Richard, even older in 1680. It seems improbable, if not impossible and ridiculous, for a man in his eighties to bequeath property to an even older brother. Obviously, I needed to rethink the situation. Without knowing what happened to Marie's son, I could not be sure which line I descend from.

I had been agonizing about what may have happened to him ever since discovering Richard Hannes, baptized 1635, and his brother, John, baptized 1625, in the Swerford parish records. Everything about these Swerford brothers, Richard and John, fit perfectly with what I knew about my Richard. Their grandfather, John/1 of Swerford, must surely be my ancestor, I thought. But he had absolutely no visible connection to Marie and her son, John, who could also be my Richard's grandmother and father. Without some evidence of a marriage and children or a burial for Marie's son John, I could not be sure he was my Richard's father. But, in spite of my searching every possible archive and record office again, no appropriately timed vital record for John Heynes appeared.

In my confusion, I went back to re-read the old wills and the old books again. I created a timeline. I jumped to conclusions and assumed possibilities without evidence. I made charts of possible connections. Richard Haynes of Grafton Flyford who died in 1555 could have been the father of Richard Handes of Henley in Arden who died before October, 1606. And Richard Handes of Henley in Arden could have been the father of John/1 Hannes who was buried at Swerford in 1607. The names and dates I was sure of did fit together conveniently except for their spellings and locations; but I knew that finding consistent spelling of family names in old records was impossible, and I had found probable reasons for their migrations. Large land owners had been getting rid of the tenants and their houses so they could fence in more acreage for sheep pasture. Whole families had to find new places to live as well as new ways to make a living.

But in spite of these considerations, the Swerford Hannes line had no time or place in which I could fit Marie Heynes and her son, John, of Kings Sutton. Not only did I fail to find a burial for Marie's son, evidence of a marriage or children also eluded me. He seemed to disappear sometime after serving as executor of his mother's will in 1634. I realized, of course, that many old records were lost due to any number of reasons, the most likely being the civil war during those particular years, and I might have to let go of my need to find a burial for him. Even though they both exhibited glaring facts connecting them to my Richard, I still had absolutely no evidence to support a connection between the Swerford Hannes line and the Kings Sutton Heynes or Haynes line.

But wait a minute. What about land tenure. Park says that "most land tenure was dependent on 'customs of the manor' and the phrase 'according to the custom', is found time and time again in manorial records."

And they did not all have the same customs or practice the same form of tenure and dower. Since women could not own land, none of the three women whose wills are copied here bequeathed land, and one man, Richard of Helmdon, probably because he did not own the land, did not mention it in his will. But three men did have land to give, and John/1 in his 1607 will, used both primogeniture, where the eldest son was the customary heir, when he gave property at Henley in Arden to his eldest son, Richard, while using a form of Borough English inheritance when he left holdings at Knowle to his youngest son, Edward. Borough English is a form in which the youngest child, son or daughter, inherits his or her deceased mother's property.

According to Wikipedia, the internet free encyclopedia, and the law of primogeniture, "...the son of a deceased elder brother inherits before a living younger brother by right of substitution for the deceased heir." and "brothers succeed by seniority of age" subject to substitution. And also, "there are variations of primogeniture which allocate the inheritance...to "another collateral relative." John/1 bequeathed only Warwickshire property, therefore he apparently had no ownership rights to Kings Sutton in Northamptonshire. So how then, did his grandson, John/3 born 1625, come by the Kings Sutton and Astrope property he left to his younger brother and others?

It appears that John Heynes, son of Marie and Thomas of Kings Sutton, could have been *"the (grand)son of a deceased...brother"*, and may indeed have been heir to Kings Sutton property. But, as mentioned earlier, he apparently left no progeny. That would leave the inheritance of Kings Sutton property to *"a younger brother"* or *"another collateral relative,"* which as it turned out, could have been John Hannes, the eldest son of John/2 of Swerford who was baptized 2 October 1625 at Swerford. And he was *"of Kings Sutton"* when he wrote his will in 1680 and named, my Richard of Banbury, as one of his heirs.

It seems probable that John/1 of Swerford could have been brother to Marie's deceased husband, Thomas, and I believe they would have been fairly close in age. I knew that John/1's children were born between 1591 and 1605, while Thomas's children were all born before 1606 when their grandmother, Elizabeth, wrote her will. Marie and Thomas's son, John, may have been first in line to inherit Kings Sutton property, but when his apparent but unverifiable demise caused him to disappear from the records with no registered marriage or children, his "collateral relative" or the "son of a younger brother," would have been in line to inherit Kings Sutton property, that being the grandson of John/1. Further research toward finding some evidence in support of these assumptions is needed, but right now this is where I must stop.

Although I did say I was bringing this writing to an end, I can not by any means believe that research into the parentage of my Richard should end here. Many unanswered questions still stand, and I believe there might be old records and old indexes I have not seen. Most, if not all, official records were written in latin back then, and I have seen some which were impossible for me to decipher. Perhaps another Haines genealogist who is fluent in Latin and wants to take the time to analyze and prove the primogeniture of this Haines family will come along someday in the future to confirm or reject my theory.

I have organized my assumptions in the chart following. Provable facts from wills, parish records or books are in *italics*, all else is my supposition including some of their places in the family.

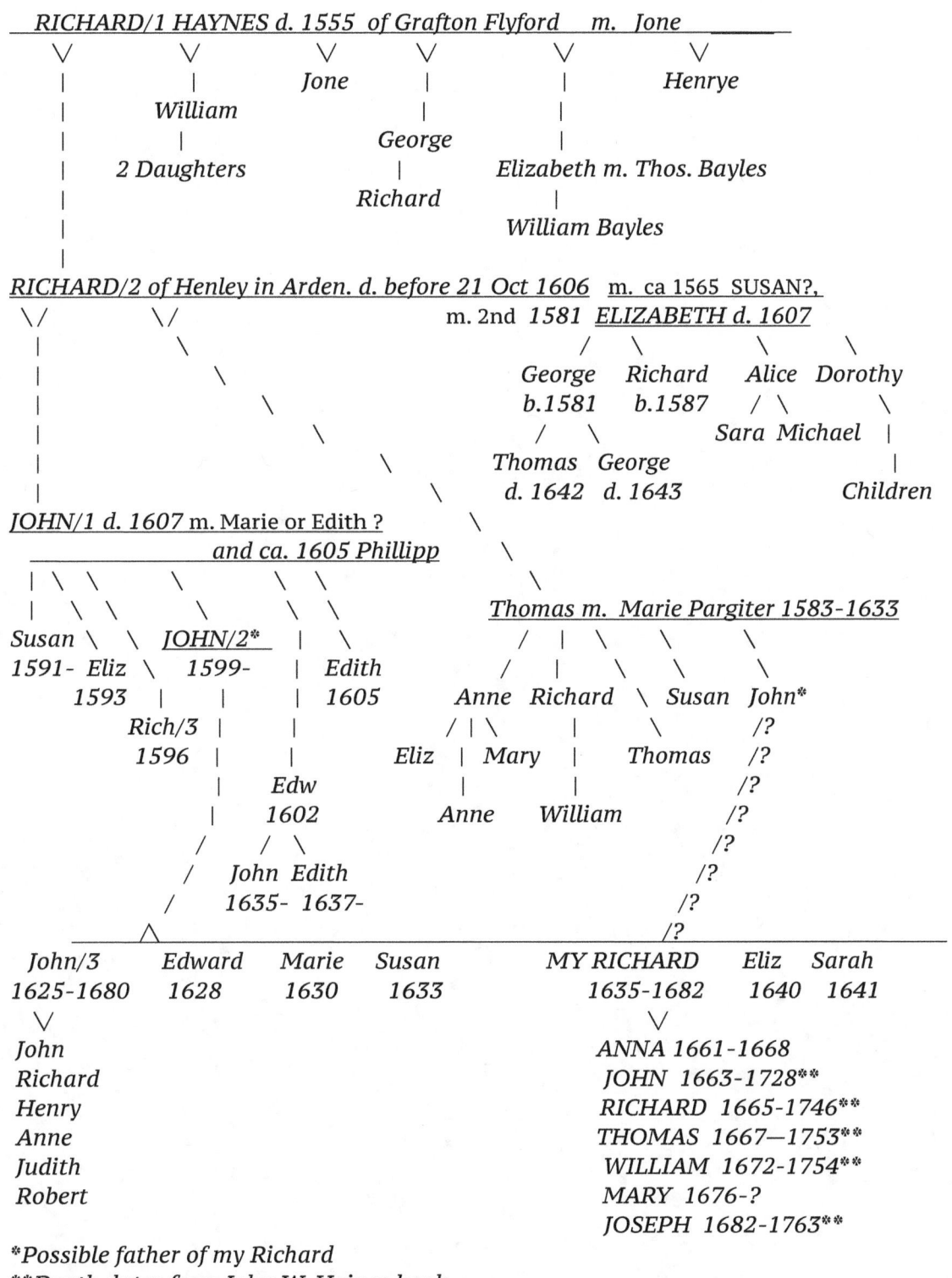

RICHARD/1 HAYNES d. 1555 of Grafton Flyford   m. Jone _____
```
   V         V         V       V          V          V
   |         |       Jone      |          |       Henrye
   |      William              |          |
   |         |              George    Elizabeth m. Thos. Bayles
   |     2 Daughters            |          |
   |                        Richard    William Bayles
   |
```
RICHARD/2 of Henley in Arden. d. before 21 Oct 1606   m. ca 1565 SUSAN?,
```
   \/        \/              m. 2nd 1581 ELIZABETH d. 1607
   |          \                        /    \      \     \
   |           \                   George  Richard  Alice Dorothy
   |            \                  b.1581  b.1587  / \      \
   |             \                        / \    Sara Michael |
   |              \                 Thomas  George            |
   |               \                d. 1642 d. 1643        Children
JOHN/1 d. 1607 m. Marie or Edith ?       \
_____ and ca. 1605 Phillipp    \
 | \ \      \        \ \              \
 | \ \       \        \ \       Thomas m. Marie Pargiter 1583-1633
Susan \ \ JOHN/2*  |   \       /  |  \    \     \
1591- Eliz \ 1599- | Edith    /   |   \    \     \
   1593  |    |    | 1605   Anne Richard \ Susan John*
       Rich/3 |    |        / | \    |    \   /?
       1596   |    |      Eliz | Mary |  Thomas /?
              |   Edw          |      |         /?
              |   1602       Anne  William      /?
              |  / / \                          /?
              | / John Edith                    /?
              |/ 1635- 1637-                    /?
_____/_____/?
```
```
 John/3    Edward   Marie   Susan      MY RICHARD    Eliz   Sarah
1625-1680   1628    1630    1633       1635-1682     1640   1641
   V                                       V
 John                                  ANNA 1661-1668
 Richard                                JOHN 1663-1728**
 Henry                                  RICHARD 1665-1746**
 Anne                                   THOMAS 1667—1753**
 Judith                                 WILLIAM 1672-1754**
 Robert                                 MARY 1676-?
                                        JOSEPH 1682-1763**
```

*Possible father of my Richard
**Death dates from John W. Haines book

BIBLIOGRAPHY

1 Haines, John Wesley, compiler. *RICHARD HAINES AND HIS DESCENDANTS A QUAKER FAMILY OF BURLINGON COUNTY, NEW JERSEY SINCE 1682.* BOYCE, VA: Carr Publishing Company, Inc., 1961.

2. Comber, John, compiler. *SUSSEX GENEALOGIES* W. Heffer & Sons, Cambridge 1933.

3 Newbottle Parish Records, Northamptonshire, England. Microfiche #6128147. Family History Library. Salt Lake City UT, USA.

4. Lind, Asbjørn P. *SLEKTSBOK FOR SØRFOLD. Utgitt av Sørfold Kommune, Norway.* 1982.

5. Fittleworth Parish Records, Sussex, England. Microfilm #0416750. Family History Library, Salt Lake City UT, USA

6. Finden Parish Records, Sussex, England. Microfilm #1364154 Family History Library. Salt Lake City UT, USA

7. *KINGS SUTTON CHURCHWARDENS' ACCOUNTS 1636-1700.* Transcribed and edited by Paul Hayter. Banbury Historical Society Volume 27. 2001

8. 1633 will of Marie Heynes. Microfilm #0092127-40. British Court Records, Family History Library. Salt Lake City, UT, USA.

9. *THE PHILLIMORE ATLAS and INDEX of PARISH REGISTERS.* 3rd ed. Edited by Smith, Cecil R. Humphrey. Phillimore & Co. Ltd., Andover, Hampshire, England.

10. 1656 Will of Richard Haines of Helmdon. Microfilm #187571. British Court Records, Family History Library, Salt Lake City, UT, USA.

11. Park, Peter B., *MY ANCESTORS WERE MANORIAL TENANTS.* Society of Genealogists, London EC1M 7BA. 1994. ISBN 0 946789 61 4.

12. 1606 Will of Elizabeth Haines of Kings Sutton. Microfilm #173601. British Court Records, Family History Library, Salt Lake City, UT, USA.

13. 1680 Will of John Haines of Kings Sutton. Microfilm #173603 British Court Records, Family History Library, Salt Lake City, UT, USA.

14. Aynhoe Parish Register, 1562-1709, Church of England. Parish Church of Aynho (Northamptonshire) (Main Author) Call Number 942.55/A2 K29c British Large Q Book, Family History Library, Salt Lake City, UT, USA.

15. 1607 Will of Johannes Haynes of Swerford, Oxfordshire, England. Microfilm #95063 British Court Records, Family History Library, Salt Lake City, UT, USA.

16. Swerford Parish Records. Oxfordshire, England. Microfiche #6142087 Family History Library, Salt Lake City, UT, USA.

17. *The RECORDS OF KNOWLE.* Copy #89, Collected by T.W. Downing, England 1914.

18. Bickley, William B.. *REGISTER OF THE GUILD OF KNOWLE in the County of Warwick, 1451-1535:* From the Original. Birmingham and Warwickshire Archaeological Society. Walsall, 1894.

19. Bird, Vivian. *A SHORT HISORY OF WARWICKSHIRE AND BIRMINGHAM.* B.T. Batsford Ltd, London, 1977.

20. *RECORDS OF THE MANOR OF HENLEY IN ARDEN,* Warwickshire. translated by Wellstood, Frederick C., M.A.. Stratford Upon Avon.MCMXIX.

21. 1555 Will of Richard Haynes of Grafton Flyford and Illegible 1548/9 John Haynes of Dornston will. Microfilm #994264. British Court Records. Family History Library, Salt Lake City, UT, USA.

22. Turner, Hillary L. *OXFORDSHIRE, A Look at the Past.* Plotwood Press, Allenton, Derby, England, 1997.

23. Illegible will of unknown Haynes of Inkbarrow. British Court Records, Warwickshire, England. Film #932932, Family History Library, Salt Lake City UT.

24. *SURVEY OF THE PARKE OF SWERFORD.* Levy List, Parchment Roll. Oxfordshire County Archives, England

25. Howard-Drake, Jack. *OXFORD CHURCH COURTS Depositions 1592-1596.* Oxford County Council, Oxfordshire, England, 1998